SUMMER
COTTAGE COMMUNITIES

T0273992

SUMMER COTTAGE COMMUNITIES

CHAUTAUQUAS, CAMP MEETINGS AND SPIRITUALIST CAMPS

PETER SWIFT SEIBERT

PHOTOGRAPHY BY JANE SWIFT SEIBERT

THE
History
PRESS

Published by The History Press
Charleston, SC
www.historypress.com

All images are from the author's collection unless otherwise noted.

First published 2024

Manufactured in the United States

ISBN 9781467156882

Library of Congress Control Number: 2023950639

For Mary and Jane, who have always made their father so very proud.

CONTENTS

PREFACE

So, it all began in 1985 with my mother taking me out on a warm summer's evening to visit this place called Mount Gretna, where there was a theater and a fabulous ice cream parlor known as the Jigger Shop. While I don't remember the play or if I had a Jigger that night, I do recall being amazed by the surrounding community. I started working in 1980 as a tour guide at a historic house museum and was in a state of rapture about Victorian architecture. Suddenly, I found myself in a community filled with dozens of Victorian cottages. The variety was endless, and I was hooked on the Pennsylvania Chautauqua. A few years later, literally by accident, I wandered across Pinch Road and discovered a whole other community of equally impressive Victorian cottages: the Mount Gretna Campmeeting.

It was in the fall that same year that, as a budding American studies major at Dickinson College, I took a class called "American Intellectual and Social History." Taught late on Thursday afternoons by the white-haired and soft-spoken Dr. Warren Gates, the class was not particularly popular among my fellow students, who had come to college to see how much beer they could start drinking on a Wednesday and sober up by the following Tuesday. During the semester, Dr. Gates lectured about the importance of the Chautauqua movement as a disseminator of intellectual ideas ranging from progressivism to Darwinian thought. His lectures hit a note with me, and I began to read about Chautauquas on the side.

Fast-forward a bit to my first job as a nonprofit executive director. I was, at the ripe old age of twenty-one, appointed director of the Historical

Society of Dauphin County in Harrisburg. With wide-eyed curiosity, I dove into the treasure-trove of artifacts and documents that were in the society's collections and found that they had been ignored for many years. One of the first things I came across was the original 1889 minute book for the Pennsylvania Chautauqua. It had ended up in the society's collections because the original secretary who kept the minutes considered the book his own property and kept it over the years. His family eventually donated it to the historical society, and thus, it languished in the vault until I found it. I remember calling up my friend Charlie Oellig and mentioning the discovery to him. Charlie told me there was a fellow named Jack Bitner who had just written the definitive history of Mount Gretna and would love to see the minute book. A few phone calls later and into my office rushed Jack to see the minute book. He devoured the contents and then, with a glimmer in his eye, looked up at me and spoke the phrase that every historian wants to utter: "I got it right."

I spent many hours with Jack in his cottage at Gretna, and eventually, we arranged for the minute book to come home, where it now rests in the collections of the Mount Gretna Area Historical Society, a group I was proud to help found. Over the succeeding decades, I met many fellow cottage community buffs and even bought and then sold a cottage at Mount Gretna.

When I returned to the Mid-Atlantic from professional stops in Wyoming, Virginia and New Mexico, I found myself again visiting Mount Gretna. The magic was still there, and soon, we were spending time discovering new communities all over the region. This book was an outgrowth of that forty-year quest to explore these magical communities.

Collingswood, New Jersey
October 4, 2023

ACKNOWLEDGEMENTS

Having lived and worked in many areas of the country throughout my career, I've always found myself drawn back to the cottage communities that were part of my youth. My wife, Kim, and daughters, Jane and Mary, indulged this passion and became my guinea pigs for testing out all my intellectual excesses in writing this book. Their love and affection have carried me during this process. Dr. Irwin Richman, professor emeritus of American studies and history at Penn State University, has been my lieber meister for decades. He has taught me much, including how to think, and I am forever indebted to him.

For the last twenty years, regardless of where I am or what I am doing, there has always been a weekly e-mail exchange with my brother, Dr. Wade Seibert. While separated by age and distance, we have always found time to write to each other. When we aren't discussing the merits of different types of chicken corn soup (white or yellow corn), he is always providing me with gentle yet firm guidance and thought on the ideas in this book.

I also want to thank, in no special order, friends and colleagues who have helped me exercise the greatest of all muscles—the human brain—throughout the decades. This list includes Reverend Dr. Wayne Mell, Chris Fritsch, Matt Webster, Matt Fortino, Dave Posavec, Wendell Zercher, Ted Wiederseim, Justin Jackovac, Craig Bruns, Mike Flynn, Carmela Quinto, Michael J. O'Malley III, Tim Sutphin, Skip Ferebee, Fred Buch, Michael Barton, Fritz Fischer, Linda Salvucci, Bruce Bazelon,

Sue Hanna, Charlie Oellig, Carl Dickson, Scott Seibert, Linda Witmer, the late John J. Snyder Jr., the late Gerry Lestz, the late Johnny Neidinger, the late Jack Bitner, my cowboy doppelgänger Keith Seidel and Chris Dezzi. You have been and always will be my friends.

1

AMERICAN PHENOMENA

Chautauquas, Camp Meetings and Spiritualist Camps

The tall figure of a man stood and faced the audience on a sultry summer evening beneath a gigantic striped tent. Dressed in a dark suit and with a water glass on a nearby table as his only prop, the speaker strode forward and, without missing a beat, began to speak. Tonight's program, titled "The Prince of Peace," was one of his favorites to deliver. He already knew, as did most in attendance, that the speech would electrify the crowd and bring them to their feet with thundering applause. This program was one of dozens of similar speeches that he was delivering that summer in small towns from Pennsylvania to Colorado. He was living his life from a suitcase, and his booking agent loved him, since he traveled light, had few demands on lodging and food and always delivered to a standing room–only audience.

The speaker was none other than William Jennings Bryan (1860–1925), the three-time Democratic nominee for the presidency who was widely regarded as the most gifted orator of his generation. Bryan's rise as a national political force came from both his populist messaging and deep religious convictions. As a native of Illinois and an advocate for farmers, he was particularly beloved in the Midwest and rural areas.

Unlike presidential candidates from earlier in the nineteenth century, who stayed at home and ran their political campaigns from their front porches, Bryan was continually on the road. He spoke with equal fervor to audiences in small western mining towns and those in packed theaters in eastern cities. Moreover, having run for the presidency three times, Bryan had his favorite

Left: William Jennings Bryan, arguably the most gifted orator of his time, was also the most popular speaker at Chautauquas across the country.

Below: Speaking to a packed house and without the benefit of a public address system, Bryan's vocal power can only be imagined. In 1907, when this photograph was taken, he was speaking in Chautauqua, New York.

14

venues, and they were neither the grandest nor largest of spaces. Rather, he loved those intimate settings where his near–religious revival style of speaking would bring the crowd to its feet. At the top of his list of favorite destinations were the summer cottage communities. They represented a dense gathering of generally well-educated people who came to listen and learn. It was an ideal proselytizing ground for a populist politician like Bryan.

The roots of the cottage communities, camp meetings, Chautauquas and spiritualist camps stretch back to the years after the Civil War, when people began to explore the notion of "taking a vacation." Today, we assume the simple notion that everyone must take a summer vacation. Whether rich or poor, one needs to get away at least once a year, ideally in the summer when children are out of school. Yet vacations were a relatively modern creation for most Americans at the time.

Before the Civil War, most Americans were bound by their professions to the towns where they worked. For city and town workers, this meant living and working in a high-density area where vast numbers of both humans and animals were eating, sleeping and pooping in proximity. Factor in the lack of consistent food refrigeration and public sanitation, and the result was a life that would have been short and smelly. Yellow fever, dysentery and a host of other illnesses brought about by the lack of sanitation could kill as fast as a runaway carriage or house fire. Thus, it was important for many living in the city to be able to find time to escape the worst of the heat, smells and risk during the summer by going to the country.

The notion of summer country retreats began among the rich living in Philadelphia. In the eighteenth and early nineteenth centuries, those who could afford it escaped to live in their summer homes along the Schuylkill or Delaware Rivers. Both rivers were cool and breezy in the summer and relatively close to the city for business purposes. Originally, the Schuylkill River was the favored choice, particularly during the yellow fever epidemic in the eighteenth century. By the early 1800s, however, many Philadelphians were looking north to the Delaware River. Among the most navigable of eastern rivers, the Delaware River served as the geographic boundary between Pennsylvania, New York, New Jersey and Delaware. Peaceful and bucolic, not prone to flooding and with a strong enough current to wash effluvia away, the river was ideal for summer retreats.

In addition, in what may be the first case of urban renewal, one of the first Delaware River towns to be "developed" for summer recreation was Bristol, Pennsylvania. Settled originally as a Quaker trading port during the 1600s, the town's business interests were supplanted by the growth of much larger

Philadelphia to the south. The town went from hub to backwater in short order. It remained quiet until it was rediscovered by prosperous Philadelphia merchants, who soon began buying up properties along the river. Tearing down the old houses, they constructed summer homes and bathhouses.

> *What a scene the wharf must have presented as the daily boats arrived, bringing the throng on pleasure bent; race track touts, and their gaudily dressed dames, gamblers, sports of all kinds along with the merrymakers out for a day in the country, with here and there a quiet and dignified Quaker arriving to do business.*[1]

This twentieth-century narrative captures the spirit of the changing community, although there is a bit of hidden irony in the prose. Most of the wealthy who, in the nineteenth century, came to build summer cottages in Bristol were descended from sober Quakers. Money from trade with Asia had fueled the local economy and created a generation of former Quaker (now Episcopalian) merchants who wanted to get away for the summer. Their summer season began in April, when the servants arrived to open the house and prepare it for the family. By May, the family had relocated to the house for the summer. The process was reversed as the family returned to the city in the fall.

By the Civil War, as modes of transportation significantly improved, the affluent families began to set their summer cottage dreams farther away. Travel, first by boat and then later by train, enabled the rich to move farther afield. Communities like Castine, Maine; Newport, Rhode Island; and Jekyll Island, Georgia, would become the new summer haunt for families from the big cities. Each of these new summer communities drew individuals from different parts of the country. Newport, for example, was the haunt of New Yorkers and Bostonians. Coastal Maine became the summer playground for Philadelphians. So strong were these ties that modern families still follow these patterns of summer vacationing that harken back to the nineteenth century. An example is the now-century-old joke that Pennsylvanians refer to coastal Maine as "Philadelphia On-the-Rocks." The reference of course is to both the rocky shores and the prodigious amount of alcohol drunk by Philadelphians during their summer in Maine.

As the nineteenth century progressed, the numbers of summer "vacationers" in these destinations grew exponentially. Upper-middle-class businessmen began to invest in summer cottages. There were local bank owners, small industrialists and, of course, real estate speculators. They

As pretty as a summer day, these two young ladies—dressed like twins—are attending the Pitman Camp Meeting in 1911.

could not afford to be away the entire summer. Rather, they needed to return to the city on a weekly basis in order to carry on their business. To serve them, small packet steamers plied the coastal rivers to bring them back to the city for their work. A story was told "of a certain gentleman who, when about to board the morning boat, was halted by his groom galloping up and informing him of the arrival of a new baby boy. Bowing politely the gentleman replied, 'Please present my compliments to my new son and tell him I look forward to meeting him with his mother on my return on the two o'clock boat.'"[2]

Transportation was critical for the rich and the upper middle class to expand their vacation horizons. For the middle and working classes, another change was on the horizon. In the years following the Civil

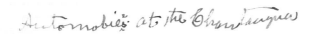

The automobile changed the summer cottage movement dramatically. Once dependent on trains, it allowed visitors to come and go as they wished. Of course, the biggest challenge, as seen in this postcard, was where to put all the cars.

War, populist political pressure was applied to state legislatures to adjust the workweek for all laborers. In 1867, the Illinois legislature passed a groundbreaking law that mandated employers provide an eight-hour workday. Over the next twenty years, public workers followed by those in the private sector gradually moved to an eight-hour workday. Paid vacations, originally reserved for white-collar workers, soon followed for many Americans. President William Howard Taft, in 1912, proposed legislation to provide two to three months of vacation for all workers. His plan failed to gain support in Congress, but the proverbial genie was out of the bottle. By World War II, most businesses were providing some type of paid vacation. These changes meant that most Americans could now not only take a vacation but also do so for a week or longer.

The choice of location for vacations was also changing. In the colonial world, God's will was always manifest, and whether by a simple bee sting or a massive hurricane, you or a loved one could be struck down in the blink of an eye. In particular, the more rural one lived, the greater the risk. Cities offered protection in the form of few animals and natural threats and better access to care. This dichotomy between the dark and fearful woods and the "city on a hill" was an integral part of life in the seventeenth and eighteenth centuries.

By the first decades of the nineteenth century, these views were starting to change. Romantic writers like Henry David Thoreau espoused more of a symbiotic relationship between man and nature. Sitting in the woods surrounding Walden Pond, Thoreau wrote these famous words:

> *I went to the woods because I wished to live deliberately, to front only the essential facts of life, and see if I could not learn what it had to teach, and not, when I came to die, discover that I had not lived.*[3]

For Thoreau, the woods were a place to go to think and to learn. Once there, one experienced nature by living and learning from it. Artists like Thomas Cole, Thomas Doughty and Asher B. Durand captured on canvas the Hudson, Delaware and Susquehanna River Valleys. Magnificent landscapes with towering mountains and broad rivers were the hallmark of their work. The artists included majestic waterfalls, magnificent sunsets/sunrises and huge stands of trees as physical manifestations of the power of nature. Yet amid this bucolic beauty, there was always the lurking question of man and mortality. In most of these paintings, somewhere in the foreground, were tiny figures posed next to trees that had been destroyed by lightning. The juxtaposition of man and a blasted tree was a reminder of both our insignificance in the grand scheme of things and random power of nature to affect our lives.

Architect Andrew Jackson Downing, the father of summer cottage design, wrote about these connections between man and nature through architectural design. He favored the Gothic style, as he saw parallels between the towering pointed spires of pine trees and those of his buildings. And of course, there was the obvious connection between those spires and the divine. The spires pointed toward the divine and also reminded the residents of the importance of the church in their lives.

The nineteenth century was also a period of immense leaps forward in popular education. Common school legislation established public education as a norm in most communities. While universal literacy was still on the horizon, more Americans were graduating high school. By the end of the century, adult learning was becoming popular, as people sought classwork long after formal schooling.

As the length of formal schooling changed, alterations occurred in the curriculum. Learning, regardless of the subject, was understood as a gift from the divine. Thus, secular science and religious theology were considered equally valuable. Moreover, to not "learn" was thought to squander a fundamental gift from God. So, where might one go to both be part of God's nature and also engage in the pursuit of God's gift to man, the quest for knowledge? The answer rested in the Chautauquas.

The story begins in 1873 around a small lake called Chautauqua in western New York. There, on the site of a Methodist camp meeting, a small group of men came together to create a summer institute of structured learning. Their plan was first to address the needs of Sunday school teachers. As the program grew in popularity, the content expanded to the broader notion of continuing adult education. The idea proved to be a case of the right thinking at the right time. Within a decade, the newly named Chautauqua Institute had become the largest nonacademic learning program in the United States. Initially open to Methodist Sunday school teachers, the program spread to other Protestant denominations and then snowballed to include an even larger mass of adult learners from across the East Coast.

The program proved to be so successful that dozens of daughter Chautauquas were soon established. By the end of the century, the movement had reached the Rocky Mountains, and towns from New England to the heartland had Chautauquas. Structurally, there were two types of Chautauquas. The first were permanent communities, such as the mother Chautauqua in New York and the Pennsylvania Chautauqua at Mount Gretna. These consisted of cottages, public buildings and open park spaces that were constructed within a formal town plan. The more common, albeit ethereal, type was the tent Chautauqua, which was run in a farmer's field or a fairground for a short period during the summer. At the center was a massive tent for programs. Around the exterior of the central tent was a gridded system of kitchens, dining tents and personal tents designed to provide some of the comforts of home. Run like a combination of a tent church revival, a circus and Woodstock, these Chautauquas brought families together to share, laugh and learn together.

While they were founded to provide Sunday school teacher training, the Chautauquas soon expanded to offer a wide range of secular programs. By the early twentieth century, they were immensely popular and were considered *the* place for aspiring politicians, budding poets, highly trained orchestras and theatrical troupes to perform. However, they were not alone. As the Chautauquas chose a secular path, there was an even larger summer program for those who sought spiritual enlightenment. Those were the camp meetings.

The history of the camp meeting movement is spiritually rooted in the tent revivals that sprang from both the First and Second Great Awakenings. These two religious movements stretched across more than two hundred

Summer on the porch of a cottage at the Pennsylvania Chautauqua in Mount Gretna in the 1890s.

years and were critical in the shaping of the Protestant tradition in America. The First Great Awakening occurred during the early 1700s and was a call to all the faithful to both demonstrate their personal repentance of sin and pledge to return to the traditional teachings of the church. The Second Great Awakening of the 1830s revived the earlier call for the repentance of sin but then pressed on the faithful to witness their faith through evangelism. Both Great Awakenings were fundamentally populist in character. Thus, whether they were held in a forested grove or beneath a tent, believers gathered for Bible readings, sermons and hymn singing. These gatherings today are called camp meetings or tent meeting revivals.

Tent revivals would sometimes last a single night and could last perhaps as long as a week. Camp meetings were much longer, and their programs included lectures, recreational opportunities and classes. Attendees could stay in tents or, if the camp meeting was of sufficient size, build a cottage. While tent revivals moved frequently based on their audience, camp meetings stayed in the same spot, often for generations.

Within the Mid-Atlantic region, the Methodist and Evangelical United Brethren Churches were the leaders of camp meetings. Between the two denominations, they operated more than one hundred camp

Shown in this image are tents surrounding a newly constructed cottage at a camp meeting somewhere in Pennsylvania. The reverse of the photograph has a notation from the photographer about being frustrated how the tents appeared around his cottage seemingly in the middle of the night and out of nowhere.

meetings from large facilities in places like Ocean Grove, New Jersey, to smaller facilities in places like Island Grove, Mexico, and Juniata County, Pennsylvania. The original purpose of the camp meetings was to test the waters in a given region to determine whether there was sufficient support to warrant a new congregation. A tent camp meeting was first held, and if enough people came, a denomination could either build a permanent cottage camp meeting or construct a new church.

The one complicating factor for the denominations was that most camp meetings were built on donated land. While free land is a good deal, it does not necessarily allow camp meetings to be situated in the area of greatest need. As a result, there often is a very high density of camp meetings in limited areas. For example, the New Jersey camp meetings at Seaville, Pitman and Malaga were all constructed less than thirty miles from each other during the span of just fifty years. They were surprisingly successful in their day, and two of the three remain as church camp meetings.

There was an interesting offshoot of the camp meetings that focused on not the souls of the living but rather communicating with the dead. These were the spiritualist camps. Born from the Victorian era's fascination with death and the afterlife, spiritualist camps were both a place for grieving family members to find common catharsis and a place to speak with the dead. The process was simple: participants would attend séances led by mediums who would go into a trance and connect with their spiritual guide. Attendees would ask the spirit guide through the medium specific questions. In turn, the spirits would communicate with the living by speaking through the medium, rapping answers to questions on tables or perhaps even appearing before them as physical manifestations.

The power of belief is central to the spiritualist experience, and participants genuinely believe that they can obtain answers from those who have died. It is a belief system that was codified by the formal spiritualist churches. Today, most of the surviving spiritualist camps have churches that are affiliated with the National Spiritualist Association of Churches. The association offers a structure to its members that bridges the formality of worship services with the informality of spiritualism. Today, there are approximately 114 member churches in the association.[4]

The spiritualist camps were much smaller than and not as well-known as either the Chautauquas or camp meetings. They were operated by single mediums whose charismatic abilities attracted large numbers of followers. Often, these mediums and their financial backers would purchase a building or camp site to provide them a permanent home. The best-known spiritualist camp is Lily Dale, located in western New York, just a short distance from the mother Chautauqua. Looking superficially at both communities, one could not really tell much of a difference. Both have cottages, hotels, dining halls and program spaces. Nevertheless, the purpose and beliefs of the two communities could not be further apart. For example, cottage ownership in Lily Dale is restricted to only those who have been tested and found to be legitimate practicing mediums.

In our purportedly modern and secular world, the popularity of spiritualism remains high. When spiritualism is married with other movements, such as Wicca, its number of believers is dramatic. The spiritualist camps were an important part of that story and remain a unique manifestation of the cottage community world.

At their heart, all the summer cottage communities shared common elements of programming and structure. First, there was the need to provide comfortable accommodations for participants and speakers. The success of

The Putnam Cottage was located in the spiritualist community of Lake Pleasant, Massachusetts. Here, attendees could attend séances or hear lectures on topics ranging from women's suffrage to theosophy.

the summer programming came from hiring both good speakers and those who presented consecutively during a week or over the span of a summer. This meant that the organizers had to find a place for people to sleep. While altruistic in their concerns, they also realized there was additional revenue to be had, as hotel owners would say, with "heads in beds." The problem was what kind of accommodations could they provide? If one was renting a farmer's field for a few weeks, the housing had to be temporary, but if the land was owned, the sky was the limit.

At the earliest camp meetings and Chautauquas, the planning committees rented out tents for participants. This worked well in the beginning, but they were both a tad buggy and also difficult to maintain and manage. Over time, as each community acquired real estate, the tents were upgraded, first by adding platforms underneath to keep people off the bare ground. While this was a definite improvement, tented platforms were still not ideal for month-long summer living. There was a serious public sanitation issue that often taxed the community's resources.

Therefore, the communities encouraged the building of wood-frame cottages around a grid of common streets interspersed within a network of parks or gardens. The communities historically chose two paths for managing the permanent cottages. The first and most widespread was having the land held by the community association or stockholders. Intended residents paid annual rent and owned only the cottage buildings. The second model that dominates today in the surviving communities is private ownership of both the house and grounds. Concurrent with the building of the cottages was the construction of hotels and dorms to provide for families and singles who did not have access to a cottage. For small communities, this could simply be a single boardinghouse, while in large communities, like Eagles Mere, there were often multiple large hotels.

With all this new construction, it is interesting to note that many cottage communities did continue to offer tents and platforms as accommodations. Despite the tents' lack of amenities, the nostalgia for the old style lived on in at least one community. Ocean Grove along the coast of New Jersey still provides for tented platform living. While it remains quite the novelty, modernity has intervened. Today, residents have constructed small sheds as part of the platforms to ensure privacy and security.

Critical to the success of all the communities was access to transportation. Until the advent of the automobile, trains and carriages were the only ways of getting to cottage communities. These modes of transportation, however, required extensive infrastructure. Train tracks and stations had to be built. However, the railroads were not anxious to spend money for just seasonal attendance unless the volume of visitors during summer was sufficiently high.

The cottage communities relied on smaller short lines that connected them to larger towns. In most cases, these rail lines were private, although a few cottage communities had their own investors who helped found the short lines that provided local access. The goal was to have the line link up with one of the larger railroads. The largest was the mighty Pennsylvania Railroad (PRR) that provided seamless transportation from Chicago to New York and all points in between.

The PRR was not alone, as there were also the Reading Railroad and the Baltimore and Ohio Railroad (B&O). All of these railroads should ring a bell for board gamers, as they are key properties in the game *Monopoly*. The game was originally set in Atlantic City, New Jersey. These three rail companies, along with numerous "short" lines, connected Atlantic seaboard vacation destinations with the big eastern cities. At the opposite end of public transportation were some of the smaller communities, such as Mount Lebanon. There, local trolley service provided access for day visitors and seasonal residents.

Trains and trolleys were the lifeblood of the cottage communities, but they had a problem: they all ran on Sundays. According to scripture and enforced by cottage community association boards, the Sabbath was a day of rest and quiet. Noisy, busy trains were anathema to the camp meetings. Yet for visitors, particularly day-trippers, Sunday access was critical for both their attendance and the economic benefit they brought to the community. One solution was to have trains stop at a nearby town and then use local horse and wagon dray service to bring guests to and from the communities on Sundays. At Pitman Camp Meeting in New Jersey, local carriages made more than one thousand carriage trips on one single Sunday to move people to and from the trains in the next town. This was clearly untenable, and over time, pressure mounted to allow Sunday rail service. The power of convenience and lost revenue ultimately prevailed, and by the 1920s, the communities were welcoming Sunday rail service.

The success of the cottage communities was very much a result of the changing world of the nineteenth century. They flourished because of the railroads and the new desire by many Americans to travel away from their homes on vacation. Set in beautiful rural spots, they became a natural draw for urban residents and workers. They appealed to those who sought knowledge through adult education. However, of greater importance, they were communities where the residents shared common values and beliefs.

In saying that, however, the cottage communities were perfect anachronisms. They existed solely because of modern technological advances that enabled people to have the time and money to travel. Yet they espoused a return to nature. The programming they offered embraced, as

This photograph of an 1880s camp meeting offers a window into the large number of people who could attend a tent camp meeting or Chautauqua.

gifts from God, both scientific and theological topics. Yet over time, church and secular education divided on the topic of Darwinian evolution.

Engineers and planners purposefully designed cottage communities. Yet they were intended to appear as free flowing, in harmony with the natural world. Structured and wild at the same time, they represent the inconsistencies in all of our lives and thus become like macaroni and cheese, the ultimate comfort food.

2

IN THE SUMMERTIME

Cottage Communities

G rowing up in the 1970s, I was frequently invited by friends to go to their parents' summer cottages along the Jersey Shore. The coasts of New Jersey, Delaware and Maryland have historically been among the national hotspots for summer seaside vacations. Because this is such a large area, there are highly subjective and epically strong opinions about the best locations in it. Debates raged among my friends about which beach had the highest-quality sand for building sandcastles or the best-tasting saltwater taffy. School recesses were filled with chatter about the tricks to be employed to win at Big Gorilla Miniature Golf or the best techniques needed to body surf in the waves. It was the stuff of preteen life that probably still occurs today.

Summer beach cottages are of two types. First are the large houses that families rented for a week or longer. Second are the bungalow colonies that had small cottages arranged around a central court. These are not to be confused with the Jewish bungalow colonies of the Catskills, although they are similar in concept. One moves in for a week or longer, with the price of the house being determined by how far the walk is to the nearby beach.

Differing from the rest of our gang in school, my best friend and his family did not have a shore cottage; rather, they rented a summer house in the Pocono Mountains. Located in northeastern Pennsylvania, the Poconos were an old destination favored by families, retirees and newlyweds. The surrounding mountains were carved from the same ancient geologic mountain range as the Catskills and Adirondacks to the north. There, the recreational opportunities

ENJOYING THE PROVERBIAL LIFE OF RILEY AT LAURENCE HARBOR, N. J. BUNGALOW COLONY

Bungalow colonies sprang up along the New Jersey shore beginning in the first decades of the twentieth century. Purely recreational, they were popular with city families looking for an inexpensive beach getaway. In this image, several families have set out their lawn chairs and potted plants and are now ready for some serious relaxation.

included lake swimming, miniature golf and the occasional town or county fair. The feel was different here, as the lakes were colder, the beaches rockier and nature, among the woods, was very close to the cabins. The cottages tended to be built in clusters, like beachside bungalow colonies are built around cul-de-sac compounds. Families rented one or more on a weekly basis and usually went the same week every year.

Having grown up in an older family (my grandparents were born in the nineteenth century), I learned at an early age that there were vastly different approaches to summer vacations. Most of my grandparents' generation grew up spending longer seasons at the summer cottage. They planned to be away for most if not all of the "season." Defining the season was also generational. It was assumed to begin around May 1 and continued to September 1. However, an older ethos holds that the summer cottage season should conclude no later than July 4. Why? Because the heat of the summer is so great after that date that families should plan to go to cooler destinations.

Another part of summer vacation life for children was summer camp. Beginning in the early twentieth century, families sent their children to summer camps as a wholesome place to be away with others of their own age. These were not day camps like we see today; rather, they ran for large chunks of the summer season. They were billed as healthy and educational experiences for children under the supervision of adults who ensured that everyone stayed healthy and safe. For families who owned or rented their own cottages for the summer season, this also meant that there were often waves of children who arrived and departed at various times.

Husbands who worked also had challenges getting to their cottages. For a choice few, they could take off the entire season. Most, however, fell into a cycle of commuting to and from the cottage, depending on the days of the week they worked. If this worked, the ideal schedule began with a departure from the city to the cottage on Friday afternoon followed by a corresponding return to the city late on Sunday. During the week, husbands would stay at home or, if they were lucky, at a private club with rooms.

The biggest decision about summer cottage living was location. Like today, the key factors were proximity to home and peer pressure from family and friends. For ocean lovers, the Atlantic coast was their destination. Within that range, however, there were defined geographic boundaries. Families living close to Philadelphia would generally go to the New Jersey shore resorts south of Little Egg Harbor. If you lived closer to New York, you would go to the northern shore communities.

Before proceeding on location, a quick aside on terminology. In the eastern United States, one goes to the shore and while there, they can walk the beach. In the western United States, one both goes to and walks along the beach. It is a subtlety of distinction, like whether a long sandwich is a grinder or a hoagie, but it is one that defines your geographic origins.

Living farther inland, vacationers shifted their summer cottage choices to one of a number of spots located in the Appalachian Mountains of West Virginia, Maryland and Pennsylvania. There were dozens of large and small spots in the mountains, but the three oldest were Eagles Mere in north-central Pennsylvania, Scalp Level and Ligonier in the Laurel Highlands and the Greenbrier and Mountain Lake Park in West Virginia and western Maryland. Like the shore communities, the mountain retreats had their geographic leanings. Pittsburghers loved Scalp Level, while Harrisburgers went to Eagles Mere and residents of Baltimore and Washington, D.C., favored Mountain Lake Park.

Whether they were along the shore or in the mountains, all of these resort cottage communities had to be near a recreational body of water. For those on or close to the coast, the Atlantic Ocean solved this problem rather handily. There was the complexity of finding the right community that had a lovely beach, gentle waves and no insects. The latter was a serious

View from Lakeside Game Lobby, Eagles Mere, Pa.

At the heart of Eagles Mere was the lake. Clear, clean and cold, mountain lakes are a rarity in the East. In this advertising postcard for a hotel, the open doors of the veranda welcome all guests, real or imagined, to come to the lake at Eagles Mere.

enough point to discount certain communities, such as Fortescue Beach, New Jersey. In the mountains, things were more challenging. Mountain streams fed by snowmelt or the occasional spring were ideal, but they were rocky and often muddy, especially in the spring and during summer storms. The ideal choice was a lake. However, naturally occurring mountain lakes are rare in the East. The once-high, craggy faces of the ancient Appalachian Mountains have long been worn down to a rolling softness. Thus, it was truly amazing when 1700s-era explorers found a clear mountain lake of great purity located high up in the mountains that ran through Sullivan County, Pennsylvania. This lake would give rise to one of the most famous mountain cottage communities in the East.

Eagles Mere, located north of Bloomsburg, Pennsylvania, in the Sullivan Highlands, is arguably one of the largest and best-known of the mountain lake communities in the East. Its history was summarized in an 1885 news story that appeared in a local paper:

Eagles Mere proper is a beautiful lake one mile and a half long and half of a mile wide, situated on the top of a spur of the Allegheny Mountains, 2,506 feet above the level of the sea. There is a small village bearing the name of the lake, and consisting of three hotels and numerous summer cottages, built on the banks of this remarkable sheet of water. The water of Eagles Mere has the peculiar greenish tint of an old ocean but is clear and free from sediment of any kind and obstacles at the bottom, in fifty feet of water, are plainly discernable.[5]

The community's history goes back to a glass-blowing business that was constructed in the 1790s. The production of glass requires fine, clean sand, and the mountain lake's shores provided an ample supply. In addition, the heavily forested surrounding mountains were a perfect source of lumber that was converted to charcoal and then used to fuel the glass furnaces. The glassworks did not last long due to the cost of transporting finished products and the challenge in finding and retaining skilled workers. Subsequently, small farms, using the already cleared land, followed the glassworks. The beauty of the lake and surrounding mountains caught the attention of several businessmen from neighboring cities. Forming themselves into a group known as the Eagles Mere Syndicate, they set out, beginning in 1877, to acquire and then develop all the land around the lake.

Eagles Mere community plans called for houses to be set on deep lots. Most of the cottages were built in the popular Shingle Style of the late nineteenth and early twentieth centuries.

Their first step was to hire civil engineer Embley Chase, who both envisioned and then implemented the town plan. Over the next forty years, Embley worked tirelessly to create and then continually revise the master plan for the town and surrounding infrastructure. His efforts culminated in the 1898 incorporation of the Borough of Eagles Mere. With Embley busy laying out the properties and streets, the syndicate began selling building lots to interested parties. The first buyers were a veritable who's who of prominent families from the nearby cities of Williamsport, Harrisburg and Bloomsburg. Bankers, judges and financiers were among those who bought lots and constructed their summer cottages. They built more than one hundred cottages in the first twenty years.

Embley Chase must have been a true workaholic. Beyond the streetscape and town plans, he also laid out the first golf course in the community. He also enacted strict ordinances to preserve the natural beauty of the community, including efforts to protect the trees that lined the lake. Finally, one of his notable visible achievements was the construction of a massive toboggan slide that sent riders flying out into the middle of the frozen lake during the winter. By 1910, Eagles Mere was *the* place for the elite of Central Pennsylvania to summer.

Of those who were connected to Eagles Mere, among the most interesting was publisher, printer, social progressive and passionate naturalist J. Horace McFarland of Harrisburg. He was part of a once-in-a-millennia generation of thinkers that included progressive naturalists like Teddy Roosevelt, John Muir and Gifford Pinchot. They sought to rethink how and where Americans would live and work in the newly modern world of the early twentieth century. At the same time, they continually looked to find ways to preserve the natural world for both the present and future.

McFarland's business, the Mount Pleasant Press, was located on a bluff overlooking the city of Harrisburg. From his office window, he could look out and see the transforming city beneath. In particular, he saw the industrial area along Cameron Street expanding rapidly with the canal, the railroad, steel plants and manufacturing facilities. Conversely, he also saw the Susquehanna Riverbank, located about ten blocks away, as an undeveloped natural area that was used as the open sewer of the city. His goal was to clean up that waste for the health of the city's residents while also creating a riverfront recreational park rather than an industrial area. McFarland found kindred sprits in socialite Mira Lloyd Dock and up-and-coming politician Vance McCormick. Together, the three advocated for a network of interconnected parks in Harrisburg based on a massive riverfront park that would provide expanded recreational opportunities for urban families, as well as ensure clean water for everyone. Their vision of the "city beautiful" to preserve existing riverfronts as parts of interconnected urban parks became a national phenomenon copied by other cities. This same preservation mindset drove McFarland to join Embley in preserving the lake at Eagles Mere.

McFarland also was passionate about encouraging a natural spirit in the design of housing and neighborhoods. As a founder of the American Rose Society, he encouraged the development of public rose gardens throughout the country. His own winter home, Breeze Hill, stood at the center of Bellevue Park. This was Harrisburg's first planned urban community, and it was laid out by prominent landscape architect Warren Manning. While Manning did not design Eagles Mere, his plans closely mirrored Embley's work.

Both Bellevue Park and Eagles Mere took existing farmland and returned it to a natural, albeit highly landscaped, appearance. Both had strict rules regarding residential plantings based on a broad understanding that the houses had to fit into the overall streetscape. In addition, they both embraced water features to create community connectivity. Eagles Mere had its lake, and Bellevue Park had a network of artificial ponds situated within the common parklands.

While McFarland was clearly a champion for both projects, Eagles Mere captured his heart. He wrote a history-cum-promotional piece in 1944, titled *Eagles Mere, and the Sullivan Highlands*. With its large size, beautiful art photography, wide margins and use of a color print set into its cover, the book is one of Mount Pleasant Press's finest printing achievements.

McFarland begins the book with a loose and almost mythical history of the community, tracing it from the Natives to William Penn and from the glasshouse to Eagles Mere. Then in the spirit of all good marketers, he pivoted his narrative and began writing about the myriad ways to easily reach Eagles Mere by train or car. He noted in particular how there was a short rail line that linked Eagles Mere to all the major railroads and destinations in the East.

The bulk of the book is about the natural beauty of the region. He waxes nostalgically about the landscape, emphasizing the ongoing healthy environment of the community. In a pointed barb toward the shore communities, he noted that "while the excitement of salt-water surf bathing may be absent from Eagles Mere, the danger is also absent."[6] He then goes on to note how clear and pure the lake water is for residents. To make his point, he commissioned and then published the results of a water quality analysis done by the Westmoreland Testing Laboratory.

While testing the water was probably not needed, the technique of using science to support his conclusions was something he knew all too well. Back in Harrisburg, McFarland had loudly advocated for a new sewage system along with the closing of open sewers along the Susquehanna River. Like the muckraker journalists of his era, McFarland used a real health threat—in this case, clean water—to drive his civic agenda. At Eagles Mere, which had the cleanest water, McFarland used his water testing to shore up public support to keep the lake clean.

The audience who came to Eagles Mere was affluent and generally well educated. As such, the town was fertile ground in which to plant the seed of a Chautauqua as well. Envisioned by Benjamin G. Welch (one of the original syndicate members) and his brother Reverend Joseph Welch, they created a summer educational program directly patterned on the model of the mother Chautauqua in New York. The idea got some energy behind it, and they soon had sufficient interest to announce the program. In August 1896, Pennsylvania governor James Beaver came to open the newly founded Eagles Mere Chautauqua.

In the first year, the Eagles Mere Chautauqua erected tents as residences for the guests and staff. By the second year, and in an effort to attract affluent guests, the Chautauqua Inn opened. The program proved so popular that

The Recreation Hall was part of the complex of cottages and other buildings constructed around the Forest Inn, and it was used by the Eagles Mere Chautauqua. Since the building was constructed in the Shingle Style, even its columns were not spared from being covered in horizontal shakes.

twelve cottages were constructed to expand the inn's capacity. Each was able rented for $150 per season. As interest built, pressure was applied to the Chautauqua board to allow private cottages to be built. The board yielded and established ninety-nine-year leases for all the additional properties. Embley Chase laid out the pattern of the cottages. To provide managed access for paying guests, a fence was added to keep out the freeloaders. Finally, the community installed electric streetlights. When the power was turned off, residents knew the curfew was in effect.

McFarland wrote that the number of cottages expanded exponentially over the next decades. In 1906, there were enough attendees for the new Chautauqua that the community of Eagles Mere Park was incorporated. The Chautauqua Inn had closed under its original management in 1906 but then reopened as the Forest Inn. Unfortunately, because of the Depression, the Chautauqua went into decline. The first thing to go was the gated entrance, as it was too expensive to maintain. No crowds meant there was no need for managed access. The programs continued to decline, so one of the large tent Chautauqua booking agencies took over programming. Even that did not boost attendance. By World War II, the Eagles Mere Chautauqua was gone. Ironically, McFarland noted in his account of the community that Eagles Mere was so attractive that many retired Chautauqua performers moved to the community.

HOTEL EAGLES MERE, EAGLES MERE, PA.

Eagles Mere, like many similar communities, had large numbers of hotels and boardinghouses that were used for short-term guests.

Lobby, Edgemere Hotel, Eagles Mere, Pa.   4B326-N

The lobby of the Edgemere Hotel is decorated almost completely in wicker furniture. A popular choice for summer cottages and hotels, wicker furnishings came in a near infinite number of forms, and their portability allowed them to be easily stored in the attic before winter.

At the community's peak in the early twentieth century, the five largest Eagles Mere hotels provided guest accommodations for more than 1,100 visitors. In addition, the community also had smaller hotels and guesthouses. Today, the large hotels are gone, but there are 143 cottages that are used by both summer and year-round residents. The community remains proprietary about access to the lake in order to maintain its preservation/conservation.

When I first visited Eagles Mere about thirty-five years ago, there were still deer that wandered the streets early in the morning. The nights were dark, and the view of the Milky Way was spectacular. Today, Eagles Mere guards its solitude well, and this has ensured that the community's original intentions remain in effect. Ironically, with climate change affecting the planet, the famed toboggan ride is now gone because the lake no longer freezes solid. Eagles Mere, however, remains as a tribute to the far-sighted leadership of its founders, who sought to carve out a summer resort in the mountains of Pennsylvania.

3

CHAUTAUQUAS

A Place, a Happening, a State of Mind

The year was 1936, and President Franklin Delano Roosevelt was facing challenger Alf Landon in his first re-election campaign. While the outcome turned out to be a landslide, with Roosevelt winning every state but Maine and Vermont, Roosevelt and Landon duked it out throughout a long campaign. Chief among the issues was the pace of world events, which were moving dangerously quickly toward war. In that year, Germany, Italy and Japan had signed treaties pledging mutual support. Adding to the tension, both Germany and Italy had also annexed several territories in what became a prequel to the 1939 invasion of Poland. With the threat of war growing, isolationist politicians—primarily midwestern Republicans—began pushing back hard on Roosevelt's global perspective.

Roosevelt decided he needed to make a major policy speech to address the Republican criticism that he was a warmonger. He knew he needed to get ahead of his opponent on this issue by laying out his own position before Landon had the chance to do so. This would entail a major policy address. But where? The key was finding a receptive audience who embraced his message and could deliver votes to him in the coming election. Roosevelt had won New York—his home state—in 1932 but only by overwhelmingly carrying the populous New York City. Western New York, with strong ties to the Midwest, remained Republican. Roosevelt had also failed to win the state's next-door neighbor Pennsylvania in 1932; although he had carried a sizeable number of the state's western counties thanks to the influence of organized labor in Pittsburgh. A spot on the western side of either Pennsylvania or New York seemed to be the best political choice for the program.

PEACE

President Franklin D. Roosevelt's
Speech at Chautauqua,
New York

AUGUST 14, 1936

"I hate war"

Left: The "I Hate War" speech by President Roosevelt was a cornerstone of his 1936 re-election campaign.

Below: The massive amphitheater or auditorium at Chautauqua was the heart of the campus. Designed to seat huge crowds, it was where both residents and day guests gathered for programs during the summer season.

The summer cottage community of Chautauqua in western New York was ideal for his policy address. While amid a Republican region, it had a sizeable number of attendees who were educated people drawn from both Pennsylvania and New York. The community had welcomed politicians from both sides of the aisle and had a strong relationship in the past with former Democratic presidential candidate William Jennings Bryan. Ever the master of the media, Roosevelt counted on friendly reporters attending via the direct train service from Chautauqua to New York City.

On the evening of August 14, Roosevelt delivered to a Chautauqua audience a fourteen-minute address outlining his view on foreign policy. While covering a lot of ground, it was his use of the phrase "I Hate War" that became the headline. In the speech, Roosevelt carefully threaded the intellectual needle of both understanding the looming European conflict that lay ahead while also not beating the American war drum too loudly to upset the electorate. Historians today regard the address as a key to Roosevelt's victory in 1936. Both locals and the summer residents came to hear the president, thereby ensuring a large crowd. Accounts note the crowds listened attentively, politely and favorably to his remarks. The press corps from New York took all of this as a sign of popular support as they reported on the speech. It was an unqualified success and was among the key factors that sent Roosevelt on to a second term.

Roosevelt was not the first president to speak at a Chautauqua. Ulysses S. Grant started the tradition and was soon followed by Presidents Garfield, Hayes, McKinley and Teddy Roosevelt. In modern times, Presidents Ford and Clinton also spoke at Chautauqua. For those hopefuls who sought the presidency but did not win, it was also a must-visit. Alf Landon, Roosevelt's opponent in 1936, spoke at Chautauqua just a few months after the "I Hate War" speech. And of course, the most famous of these presidential speakers was William Jennings Bryan, the great orator of the Chautauqua movement, who ran three times unsuccessfully for president. It was well understood by all the candidates, both winners and losers, that Chautauquas were a way of reaching educated voters and obtaining front-page coverage in the East Coast newspapers.

The story of Chautauqua begins within the leadership of the Methodist Church, which, in the late nineteenth century, was attempting to develop a training program for its Sunday school teachers. Two of the church's leaders, Lewis Miller (1829–1899) and John Heyl Vincent (1832–1920), developed a plan to bring Sunday school teachers together with faculty chosen from the academic and theological world for a formal training program. They picked the summertime, since it was convenient to both the students and presenters. The location selected was an existing church camp meeting located along the shores of Lake Chautauqua in western New York. In 1874, they held the first gathering of teachers. It was a modest success.

Looking to boost the attendance, John Heyl Vincent and Thomas Floor (the editor of the publication the *Chautauquan*) decided that what they needed was a national figure to visit who could attract the masses. They needed to find someone who would bring both respectability and lots of positive media attention. Henry Ward Beecher, the famed abolitionist, was their first choice. A brilliant orator, Reverend Beecher would have been ideal, except that he had been caught up in a public scandal over marital infidelity. The Chautauqua model was predicated on faculty and students practicing high moral standards, so Beecher was out. Vincent and Floor's attention pivoted to an even bigger name: President Ulysses S. Grant. While he was not facing re-election in 1876, Grant was out stumping to support the Republican ticket. Vincent knew the former president, as he had been a pastor to Grant when they both lived in the Midwest. The challenge was that Grant was not known to be a churchgoer. Still, the Republican Party needed him to stump for candidates, so Grant agreed to go. After a long and complex journey, Grant arrived in Chautauqua aboard the steam yacht *Josie Bell*. The media widely reported on his visit, and the resulting endorsement catapulted the new program onto the front pages of newspapers across the country. Attendance grew, and Vincent and Floor never looked back as Chautauqua became a national phenomenon.

The Sunday school training program rapidly became the largest continuing education program for adults in America. As such, it remained a cornerstone of the Chautauqua educational program for decades to come. However, as the desire of adult learning grew, new programs and schools were added. These new programs embraced secular learning in an ever-increasing number of classes and lectures. In 1879, the Chautauqua added a school of languages followed by a liberal arts school. University faculty staffed most of these programs, earning an extra stipend on top of their regular salaries.

Having all these educational programs does pose the fundamental questions of who was interested in them and for what reason. Universal literacy had become a national objective during the nineteenth century. School instruction became more complex over the decades thanks to the introduction of modern pedagogy and measured outcomes (grades). Education was important and fashionable. The result also led many to look

Guests arriving by boat were greeted by an impressive spectacle upon docking in Chautauqua. Well-dressed people walking among cottages, Greek temples and playing lawn sports suggested this was something more than a colony of ascetics.

Landscaping was an important part of the Chautauqua experience. Towering trees and well-manicured flower beds affirmed the healthy and wholesome nature of the community.

beyond a basic grammar school education. During the Civil War, Abraham Lincoln established the Land Grant Colleges/University program that allowed states great latitude in establishing schools of higher education. As a result, schools such as Penn State, Rutgers and Cornell were established to teach animal husbandry, agriculture and bee keeping as well as history, English and math. The modern college/university system was evolving. But what about those adults who either did not attend college or had received a weak secondary education? The answer was the Chautauqua movement, where, for a fee, you could attend lectures and programs taught by academic faculty during the summer.

What began as a noble endeavor to encourage teaching and learning for all soon ran into the problem of controversial topics. Darwin's theory of evolution was of course dangerous enough, but there were others. Helen Hunt Jackson's exposé *A Century of Dishonor* drew attention to the ill treatment of American Natives. Jack Reed's *Ten Days that Shook the World* presented the Russian Revolution in a positive light to Americans. The list goes on, and one would be remiss without mentioning Chautauqua alumna Ida Tarbell, whose *History of the Standard Oil Company* became a hallmark of muckraking journalism. It remains one of the one hundred greatest books of the twentieth century. While not all of these authors were Chautauqua speakers, their writings resonated throughout the curriculum. Within a decade of Chautauqua's founding, a divide between the religious and secular educational programming began to show. What started as a small crack grew into such a huge chasm that by the 1910s, the Bible Conference was listing its educational programs separately from the Chautauqua educational programs. The world had changed, and Chautaquas followed. It all sounded very controversial, and certainly, at the administrative level, these debates caused substantial heartburn for the Chautauqua boards. Yet for the average attendee, the seemingly infinite variety of programming was a veritable intellectual candy store to be sampled and enjoyed.

Chautauqua attendees participated in the program in several ways. The first and most inexpensive was by being a day visitor. One simply purchased a train or boat ticket to be there and then paid admission for the day to attend programs on the Chautauqua grounds. This was how most people experienced Chautauqua programs. These day trips proved so popular that the Pittsburgh, Titusville and Buffalo Railroad transported an estimated 300,000 day visitors to Chautauqua in a single season. The second way to attend was by spending one or more nights in one of several on-site hotels or boardinghouses. They offered a room and

The Colonnade Cottages were typical of those built at Chautauqua. They were constructed with asymmetrical façades, rambling porches and complex exterior siding and roof shingling. This look became synonymous with the cottage style.

meal service at a range of prices for guests. Finally, there was the ability to rent or own an individual cottage. Most felt this was the best way to experience Chautauqua. For the communities, cottages were a sign of permanence, since owners represented their core constituency. Coming back year after year, paying a ground rent or local taxes, the cottage owners supported the Chautauqua.

Communities throughout the country soon copied the educational and community structural model that was created at the mother Chautauqua. Halls of philosophy patterned on Greek temples were built in Chautauquas across the Midwest and up to the foothills of the Rockies. In the East, communities quickly sprang up in Pennsylvania, Massachusetts, Maryland and other states. The largest of these "daughter communities" was the Pennsylvania Chautauqua at Mount Gretna. It was located in northern Lebanon County, within a short train ride of Harrisburg, Lancaster, Lebanon and Reading.

Mount Gretna sits on the side of one of several iron-bearing rocky ridges that served as the boundary between Lancaster and Lebanon Counties. Beginning in the 1700s, iron was quarried from these hills and sent to the nearby Cornwall Furnace, where it was melted into bar iron. This was then used in making everything from hinges and kettles to cannon balls. In addition to the iron extraction, there was also a lively business of cutting trees from the ridges to be converted into charcoal.

The Coleman family, often described as America's first self-made millionaires, owned most of the land that included the quarries, iron furnaces and charcoal burning operations. The region was one of America's first industrial landscapes. Its appearance in the late 1700s was that of quarries: smoldering charcoal pits, smoky furnaces and piles of overage and waste rock. By the late 1870s, the introduction of large commercial steel and iron plants elsewhere meant Cornwall was out of date. The trees began to grow back on the hills as the landscape returned to a more natural state.

Enter Robert Coleman, who envisioned a different use for the family real estate holdings. Coleman saw opportunity in the lovely bucolic ridges covered with new trees and peppered by natural springs. While the hilly land was not suitable for farming, Coleman conceived of a large private park that took advantage of the view. He named it Mount Gretna Grove, which was derived, depending on the day, from either a Scottish town where couples went to be married or the German word for "pearl." Thanks to Coleman's seemingly limitless financial backing from his family's fortune, the new park soon became a regional destination. In 1881, Coleman created a lake by damming one of the spring-fed steams. Today, the lake is used in the summer, just as it was then, for swimming and boating, and it is the visual centerpiece of the Mount Gretna landscape.

Boat Landing, Mt. Gretna Park, Pa.

On a summer day in 1912, visitors to Robert Coleman's Mount Gretna Park could relax by taking a boat ride on the man-made lake.

Coleman understood that the residents of the small cities in the region needed some kind of outdoor recreational experience. These older communities lacked good public park systems for recreation. Mount Gretna became that ideal destination. In 1891, Coleman purchased a carousel in Philadelphia and brought it to the park to add more interest. Looking to add more attractions, he constructed a narrow-gauge railroad pleasure line that took visitors to the top of the Governor Dick, the ridge located above Gretna Grove. It was all great fun for Coleman and proved to be a savvy capital investment.

Ever the entrepreneur, Coleman learned that the Pennsylvania National Guard needed to find a new spot for its 8,500 members to drill and fight mock battles during the summer. In the past, the national guard had used the nearby Gettysburg Battlefield, but this was no longer available. Coleman recognized that all those hungry soldiers and animals needed plenty of provisions during their summer camp. Then there was the public who liked to come out for the day to see the parades and mock battles. The visitors and their horses needed to eat as well. Finally, the cherry on top was that numerous politicians and famous generals would also come to these encampments. Their presence would be a glowing endorsement for the location chosen for the national guard's encampment. All this added up to

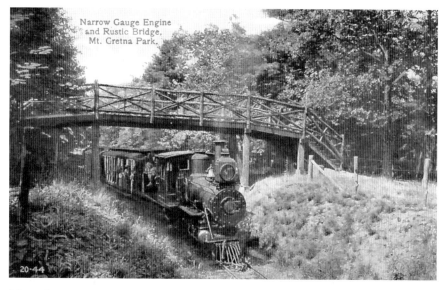

Mount Gretna Park was truly something to behold for its variety of activities, including the narrow-gauge pleasure railroad steaming beneath a log bridge.

Coleman's efforts to secure a contract to bring the national guard to Mount Gretna for its encampment. And like raindrops in summer thunderstorm, the soldiers came en masse.

The national guard of the nineteenth century was very different from today's modern citizen soldiers. In most states, national guard units were social organizations that focused on drilling and held elaborate balls. An exemplary group was the Harrisburg City Grays, whose primary task was to perform ceremonial duties around the state capital. During the nineteenth century, the national guard was rarely called into active service. On one occasion, during a particularly violent railroad strike, the Harrisburg City Grays did distinguish themselves. The story goes that purely because of their superb marching skills and precise execution of the manual of arms, they were able to cow an angry mob into submission.[7] The Grays, along with the State Fencibles, the First City Troop and their rivals—the Governor's Troop—all came for summer drill to Mount Gretna. The training was great fun for the participants and usually culminated in a grand review with the governor and other politicians. A friend of mine who enjoyed hunting for vintage glass bottles claimed the site of the encampment was one of the richest he had ever dug, particularly in the quantity of expensive wine and liquor bottles. The encampments lasted for several decades until more space was required for the tanks and artillery. As a result, the guard moved to the opposite side of Lebanon County to the newly created Fort Indiantown Gap.

Having secured the national guard contract, Coleman began to look elsewhere for other organizations to make Gretna something more permanent. In 1891, he met with a group of local religious and civic leaders who were interested in starting a Chautauqua. Patterned on the success of the mother community in New York, the new community was appropriately called the Pennsylvania Chautauqua. The idea caught on, and stock in the new Pennsylvania Chautauqua Corporation was issued and a board of directors duly elected. In 1897, Coleman formally sold the group the land that comprises the present-day community. However, never one to let moss grow on a sleepy woodland rock, Coleman also began negotiating with members of the Stoverdale Camp Meeting to move their summer program to Mount Gretna as well. One year after selling the land to the Chautauqua, Coleman sold a similar block of land to the newly established Mount Gretna Campmeeting. In doing so, he created what may be a unique phenomenon: a private park, a Chautauqua and a camp meeting—all located in the same spot.

The Pennsylvania National Guard's summer muster at Mount Gretna brought thousands of soldiers, vendors, politicians and well-wishers to the community. With this 1909 photograph, one can get a sense of what camping among the pines was like at Mount Gretna.

The new Chautauqua set out to build the needed infrastructure to support its intended programming. Among the community was constructed a massive auditorium designed and built by local architect/engineer John Cilley. Cilley, a native of nearby Lebanon, took a lesson from the structures of local barns when designing the auditorium. Realizing that a network of vertical posts rising from the floor would hinder the view of many, he devised a collar with cabling that tied the roof framing together. When ratcheted tight, the cabling provided sufficient structure to withstand most weather. Cilley's design apparently became the norm for many communities, including the Mount Gretna Campmeeting, Mount Lebanon Camp Meeting and Mountain Lake Park in Maryland. Speculation has also abounded for years about whether Ocean View and several other camp meetings also used Cilley's designs. The Chautauqua auditorium was rebuilt after a snowstorm damaged it in 1993, and it remains at the heart of the Pennsylvania Chautauqua.

The first cottages were constructed close to the auditorium along streets named for Ivy League universities. The naming choice is significant, as it re-enforced the notion that Chautauquas were places of higher learning

Top: The Hall of Philosophy was one of several buildings constructed in the Chautauqua to provide space for classrooms and smaller programs.

Bottom: Today, this building is a gift shop, but in the past, it was home to the CLSC, an organization that promoted year-round learning in the Chautauqua style.

and intellectual thought. The association built wooden copies of Greek temples to house the Hall of Philosophy and the Chautauqua Literary and Scientific Circle. The location of the community next to the nearby lake, carousel and pleasure railroad also meant it had abundant recreational opportunities for families.

Good road access to Mount Gretna was exceptional thanks to the combined voices of the camp meeting, Chautauqua and national guard and the sheer will of Robert Coleman. Carriage and, later, automobile drivers were able to access the community from Harrisburg to the west and Reading to the east. The Manheim Pike connected the town to Lancaster County to the south. To transport the national guard units, commercial rail service was built to provide linkage with the Reading and Pennsylvania rail lines. The benefit to the Chautauqua was that the community was linked to New England and the coastal South. Finally, a local trolley service provided local access from nearby towns. Thanks to this, the community finally reached the critical mass needed to become successful.

Faculty from nearby Lebanon Valley and Franklin and Marshall Colleges staffed summer programs. Religious instructors included local pastors, as well as faculty from both the Lutheran and Reformed seminaries located nearby.

A particularly noteworthy aspect of Mount Gretna was the summer theater program held inside the auditorium. The theater opened its first season in 1927 in response to a desire for more summer programming by the Chautauqua's board of managers. The first director was A.E. Scott, who was both an actor and director at the Fulton Opera House, a theater in nearby Lancaster. The theatrical productions took off and became one of the most distinctive aspects of Mount Gretna. Young up-and-coming actors like Charlton Heston had some of their first theatrical performances at Gretna Theater. In my youth, the productions were well known, and it was common for couples and families from Harrisburg and Lancaster to drive to Mount Gretna in the evening to see the latest show. For a time, there was a standing joke that Gretna Theater was where you went to see the cast members of the much-beloved former television series *M*A*S*H* Both Jamie Farr (Corporal Klinger) and William Christopher (Father Mulcahy) were regular performers. Gretna Theater continues to attract quality actors down, and it is a centerpiece of the summer season for the community.

Today, the Mount Gretna Chautauqua remains a viable and stable community, where real estate values are both high and remarkably stable. In the wake of the COVID-19 epidemic, the cottages became ideal stay-

Top: Mount Gretna was close enough to the nearby town of Cornwall that a trolley service ran between the two during the summer.

Bottom: Summer visitors who did not come by train had the challenge of finding space for their carriages and paying for the care of their horses.

The auditorium designed by John Cilley was at the heart of the Mount Gretna Chautauqua. Its use, however, changed over the years, as it moved from being a center for lectures to a home for popular theatrical productions.

at-home workspaces, resulting in a new generation of year-round residents coming to the community. The Jigger Shop, the resident ice cream parlor in Mount Gretna, remains the largest tourist draw for the community. Operating since 1895, the Jigger Shop has been the singular Mount Gretna destination for four generations of my family. It is famous for the "jigger," a massive confection defined by French vanilla ice cream with your choice of chocolate or butterscotch, marshmallow and nuts.[8] When assembled, it can be a meal unto itself. As a boy, I was told that a Soviet Union–era guide to the United States suggested only two places to visit in Pennsylvania: Independence Hall in Philadelphia and the Jigger Shop in Mount Gretna. True or not, it conveys the power of ice cream and Mount Gretna to attract even the most hardened Marxist.

In the Mid-Atlantic, the Pennsylvania Chautauqua at Mount Gretna and Chautauqua, New York, represented the most elaborate and sophisticated of these communities. A special note should be made of Mountain View Park Chautauqua, located in western Maryland. Founded in 1881, not long after the mother Chautauqua was established, it flourished through the remainder of the nineteenth century. The Chautauqua was established by five Methodist ministers and followed the New York model of offering

Herrmann Cottage, on the Chautauqua Grounds, Mt. Gretna, Pa.

The Hermann Cottage, now passed out of the original family, remains the largest private home in the original part of Mount Gretna.

Chautauqua Hotel, Mountain Lake Park, Md.

Hotels, even those located in the mountains, were challenging to heat and cool. This July 1916 postcard shows numerous windows open and blinds down as the residents and staff of the Mountain Lake Park Chautauqua Hotel attempt to stay cool.

educational programs and recreational opportunities. The success of the community was a direct result of the Baltimore and Ohio Railroad, which built a series of passenger lines into the western Maryland mountains to connect with vacation-goers in Baltimore.

Mountain View Park had a large central hotel and a series of cottages laid out on a grid system, along with an auditorium. The community probably hit its peak in the 1920s and was in steep decline by the end of World War II. The draw of nearby tourist destinations, such as White Sulphur Springs in West Virginia, took away its audience and, ultimately, its cottage owners. Today, there is year-round occupancy for many of the houses. The history of the community, however, has not been lost, and there is an annual celebration of the community's Chautauqua roots.

The Chautauquas were widespread disseminators of higher-level learning to a public who thirsted for knowledge. In particular, women who were relatively new in widely attending college could find real intellectual stimulation in the Chautauqua programs. The speakers, drawn from the liberal arts academic tradition, introduced new ideas on topics such as the theory of evolution and pan-globalism. The artistic programs inspired untrained weekend painters to expand their technical skills and horizons. The Chautauquas were where the lofty plane of intellectual thought met the runway of populism.

4

FROM TENT TO TED TALK

On any given summer day in the 1890s, a crew of burly laborers would arrive to erect a massive tent in the middle of a fallow farmer's field. Like Noah building his ark, it drew dozens of questions from the locals. Something was happening—but what? The answer came in a blitz of postcard mailers and newspaper advertisements that announced a tent Chautauqua was soon to be held. The preprinted programs promised a roster of musicians, poets and actors along with lecturers speaking on various topics and then, to cap it off, a big-name political figure. Like a traveling circus, the entire event was billed as a spectacle. Unlike a circus, however, the program ostensibly focused on educational and morally uplifting ideas.

On the appointed day, the local town was abuzz with anticipation. The Chautauqua speakers and entertainment arrived on a train, often with painted cars advertising the program. Families in the surrounding countryside would drive their buggies to the site of the giant tent, where they would pay their admission to attend the programs. For those planning to come for several days or who were traveling from a distance, tents would be available to rent and live in during the program. There was a dining area available for families. Surrounding the community were fields for grazing horses and shaded areas for storing wagons.

Each day during this education carnival, well-polished speakers, who had been honing their presentations for weeks at other identical events, would mount the stage to deliver their program. At the end, families left feeling maybe smarter, perhaps more cultured and probably quite relaxed and

Tent Chautauquas were intended for populist education and entertainment. Anyone was welcome for the price of a ticket.

satisfied by the entire experience. In a world before radio or television and with only grainy movies for competition, the tent Chautauquas were places for entertainment and fun couched in "great learning." For small communities, these programs provided both a community service for residents and a cash cow for local merchants. The model was quite simple. A local committee was established to identify and develop the infrastructure for the program. Their first and most critical task would be finding the right spot. Part begging, part strong-arming and lots of diplomacy were needed to find a good location.

The ideal spot would be several large grassy farmers' fields located along a well-maintained road close to town. They would look for a field that was free of crops, had no standing water and was close to a road. This was used for the big tent. Other nearby fields were then identified, since, in the horse and buggy era, participants needed a place to both park their carriages and graze their livestock. The carriage field should ideally have some shade cover to protect the vehicles from baking in the sun. The livestock field needed a good water source that was very close by. Moreover, of course, the key in all of this was finding fields that had grass rather than new crops or plowed dirt that would turn into mud. It was a huge task.

For many towns, particularly in county seats, the best place was the local fairgrounds. Built for the annual county fair, they were a prime choice for a tent Chautauqua, since they often included already-constructed pavilions,

The Redpath-Vawter Booking Agency sent this color postcard out in advance of one of its programs to encourage ticket sales. The speakers were politicians (William Jennings Bryan, *top center left*), scientists and clergy.

In this 1908 real photograph postcard, young and old alike watch a speaker at the Racine, Wisconsin Chautauqua. The program must have been good, since few people seem to notice the photographer.

The boy, who all last year
Boosted
CHAUTAUQUA
alone,
Brings kid sister this year,
She wouldn't stay home.

THE SWARTHMORE CHAUTAUQUAS
PAUL M. PEARSON, Director
Swarthmore, Penna.

Tent Chautauquas were family oriented, as this novelty postcard suggests.

bathrooms and other infrastructure. They also often had the benefit of being adjacent to rail lines, so trains carrying speakers, performers and tents could get there. Fairgrounds or fields close to town were also important because of their ancillary support, like having a hotel in proximity. Big-name speakers were not going to sleep in tents, so a nearby hotel with a restaurant was important.

Regardless of the location, another critical element was the ability of the management to fence and gate the Chautauqua. The town and promoters relied on ticket sales to meet expenses and make a profit. So, providing managed access was critical for the success of the programs. Of course, fencing and off-duty town constables were expensive but necessary. To allow the event to be open and unsecured was to invite financial ruin.

Once the location was determined, the second step for the local committee was to hire a professional booking agency. These commercial firms established the program, retained the talent, arranged the transportation, developed and distributed the marketing materials, provided the tents and managed ticket sales. For all this work, they also took a substantial and well-deserved share of the profits. By 1900, there were roughly a dozen talent agencies that provided Chautauqua talent. In the Mid-Atlantic region, the biggest were Swarthmore, Redpath, Vawter and Coit-Albert. Since these agencies often merged and then separated, they created a multitude of name combinations. Arranging programs was not as easy as it looked, since there needed to be a balance between the performers and the educational lecturers. The speakers needed to be well known and perhaps a bit edgy, but they could not cross the line. The latter was a challenge then, as today, since community perspectives on issues varied geographically. To read the community required great skill and the most successful booking agencies closely matched their program choices to the needs of the community. Finally, there needed to be a headliner whose name would catch the imaginations and open the public's wallets. The keynote needed to be someone whose name was on the tip of everyone's tongue. This was not a small fete, as yesterday's politicians were numerous and rarely sold tickets or filled a house.

To understand the complexity of the programs, let's look at three different tent Chautauquas held in the town of Brookville, located in Jefferson County in western Pennsylvania. The Chautauqua's programming was booked over all three years by the same firm: the Coit-Albert Agency. The firm was founded in Cleveland, Ohio, in 1913, and Brookville was among its first clients. In 1914 the keynote speaker was scheduled to be the Honorable Robert M. La Follette Sr., a populist progressive Congressman from Wisconsin. Since he was one of the most iconic figures of early twentieth-century politics, his track record can best be summarized by quoting from his official Congressional biography:

> *When asked to name the five most illustrious senators in history, a Senate committee led by John F. Kennedy included in that elite group Republican Robert La Follette of Wisconsin (1855–1925). Independent and impassioned, La Follette championed such progressive reform measures as regulation of railroads, direct election of senators, and worker protection, while opposing American entry into World War I and condemning wartime restrictions on free speech. He initiated the investigation into the Teapot Dome scandal of the early 1920s and ran for president on the Progressive Party ticket in 1924. In choosing La Follette as one of the "Famous Five" in 1957, the Kennedy committee described him as a "ceaseless battler for the underprivileged" and a "courageous independent" who never wavered from his progressive reform goals.*[9]

La Follette was a superb speaker and had been drawing national audiences on the tent Chautauqua circuit for several years. He used his position as a keynote speaker at these events not only to connect with the electorate but also to address broader political and social issues.

In 1914, La Follette was stumping across the country arguing that President Woodrow Wilson was too soft on business. His concern was that Wilson, like most prior presidents, was too beholden to corporate elites and thus was not making policies of true benefit to the United States. This message was well received, particularly in the heartland, where farmers and small businessmen saw the majority of America's wealth tied to eastern cities. In addition to his big message, La Follette was also busy stumping for fellow progressive political candidates. The 1913 election year cycle had been hard on progressive candidates, particularly in the Midwest. As a result, La Follette was dispatched to drum up support nationwide. That year, wherever he spoke, big crowds were sure to follow, and Brookville's planning

Above: The Honorable Robert M. La Follette Sr. is shown arriving at a tent Chautauqua to deliver an anticorporate message to the assembled attendees.

Left: Patriotism was clearly the theme of the 1918 Chautauquas, since the United States was at war with the Central Powers in Europe.

committee, along with the promoter, were equally thrilled to have him as their keystone program.

Three years later, at the Brookville Chautauqua of 1917, La Follette was gone. His hesitancy about the growing American intervention in World War I was no longer a popular position. While his fall from political grace would not last forever, he was not going to be a big enough draw for Coit-Albert to use him. So, they pivoted on speakers and brought to Brookville someone more in tune with America's patriotic mood. Their chosen keynote that year was the charismatic and entertaining LaSalle (Sally) Corbel Pickett. For those not familiar with her name, she was the widow of Confederate general George Pickett of Pickett's Charge fame in the Battle of Gettysburg.

While Sally Pickett's presence was seemingly at odds with the pro-patriotic fervor of the 1917 audience, she did not focus her lecture on the lost cause of the Confederacy. Rather, her program was about all the famous American generals and politicians she had known over the years before, during and after the Civil War. The list was carefully chosen and well balanced between both Union and Confederate figures. She spoke in familiar ways about Generals Grant and Lee, along with Presidents Lincoln and Davis. Further, in order to temper any concerns about her politics, she was billed as the "child bride of the Confederacy." The title suggested that she had no political knowledge of those times but was simply a youthful observer.

Sally Pickett joined a long line of Civil War–era figures who had been regularly brought out to speak before crowds on the Chautauqua circuit. Beginning in the late 1880s, there was a concerted national effort to mend the cultural, social and political rifts caused by the Civil War. Whether in writing new histories of the war or reuniting Union and Confederate soldiers at various battlefields, Americans sought to heal the wounds of the war. As a final effort to ensure that the audience understood this spirit of national reconciliation on the eve of World War I, there was also a special musical group on the program. Colonel Pattie's Old Soldier Fiddlers was a group consisting of Union veterans of the Civil War who played for the crowd a selection of patriotic music. With Sally Pickett billed along the band, the tent Chautauqua's message was of a unified country standing ready for the challenges of the upcoming war.

Two years later, in 1919, with the war won, Brookville's Coit-Albert tent Chautauqua went in a completely different direction. The program that year was labeled "the Victory Chautauqua" and appropriately featured poetry readings from Australian soldier Tom Skeyhill. A nine-piece band consisting of American World War I veterans accompanied him. While all of this was dutifully patriotic, it was clear that the audience and the promoters were looking beyond the war. Thus, the headline act was George M. Cohan's melodrama *Seven Keys to Baldpate*. This mystery comedy was clearly the crowd attractor, and advertisements for the cast and Cohan alone took up more than one-quarter of the published program.

An interesting note is that buried inside the 1919 program was the announcement of a Sunday afternoon program featuring the Fisk University Jubilee Singers. Today, this group is considered one of the most important Black musical groups from the early twentieth century. Founded in 1871 at the historically Black Fisk University, the Jubilee singers performed a capella spirituals at summer tent Chautauquas. Musicologists and historians alike acknowledge their efforts in keeping alive many spirituals dating from the slave era and Reconstruction.[10]

Music by veteran bands, soldier poets home from the front and a host of other patriotic artists were favored in the period during and just after World War I.

Their performances, while not apparently widely advertised, were in a key place in the program. Sunday afternoon was when a substantial crowd would be present. While sadly little is known about the impact of their performances in the town, their program was a harbinger of things to come.

The program was the key to building a strong tent Chautauqua program. Promoters and local committees needed to sell a lot of tickets. Add into that mix the local merchants, hotel operators, blacksmiths and others who saw their pocketbooks swell when the program came to town. However, sometimes even the program was not enough. The tent Chautauquas also needed to rely on some P.T. Barnum–inspired theatrics to make it work. One example was used by the Redpath Agency, which marketed its tent Chautauquas on a traveling circus model by having special trains painted with both its business and performers' names on the outside of the cars. The train arrived with great fanfare in a town, complete with parades and impromptu performances. It was all great fun, and the spectacle of the arrival and departure appealed as much as the program did to many.

However, change was in the air—literally—as radio became the big competitor for life lectures and concerts. The programming was the same and one did not need to leave the comfort of their home. Another game changer was the popularity of the car. Families could now travel to a tent Chautauqua and go home the same night without needing accommodations or meals. The lack of an upsell to attending a tent Chautauqua proved nearly as fatal as the radio. Then there was the impact of the Great Depression in the 1920s and 1930s. A lack of disposable income for families meant that ticket sales faltered. In the hopes of riding a new wave of "happiness rather than scholarship," the booking agencies booked more entertainment and fewer lectures. Like eating cotton candy, there was an immediate sugar rush of enthusiasm for the new entertainment focus, but it did not last long. People wanted big names, and the inability of towns and promoters to provide advance financial guarantees meant bureaus were also forced to book less well-known acts. As one scholar noted, "The country was full of third rate sopranos and second string politicians to be bought at a dime a dozen, William Jennings Bryan and Alice Nielsen, the White Hussars and the Ben Greet Players could not be picked up on any bargain counter."[11]

One by one, the speaker's bureaus failed. By the 1950s, the widespread arrival of television put the final nail in the coffin for the tent Chautauquas. What once had brought life to small towns in the Mid-Atlantic was now just a memory. Yet there was one element from these programs that survives to the present: the community lyceum. These date to the first half of the nineteenth century, when small towns would bring in speakers and programs hosted by local community groups. The key to their success was their location in public auditoriums, free from concerns about weather. Because of this, the programming was spread out over the year rather than dependent on a single week.

More educational than entertainment, these lyceums also lacked the showmanship element that had been at the heart of the tent Chautauquas. By limiting their overhead expenses, they were able to attract and pay for consistently high-quality speakers. By the 1980s, the lyceums had evolved into the modern-day community "speaker series." The only change was dropping the name "lyceum," which had fallen out of popular usage in much of the country. Like the tent Chautauqua, community speaker series have a local community civic committee that hire a talent agency to find four or five speakers to come to a local civic hall to deliver a program. The debate about how political to be remains the same as it was for the tent programs. Television figures like the late journalist Charles Kuralt, who

Ben Greet Players — Redpath Chautauqua.

THE FIRST LYCEUM: A. E. Winship

TALENT.

A Monthly Magazine of the Lyceum

REV. EZRA RIPLEY, D.D., First President of the First Lyceum
Organized at Concord, Mass., 1829

Above: The Ben Greet Players were the most popular entertainment at tent Chautauquas. Today, they are considered among the first professional acting troupes in America.

Left: The Lyceum movement was so popular that a literary magazine was founded to both promote speakers and programs and provide quasi-scholarly articles.

provided midwestern homespun, were always favored. Another equally big pool of presenters were former astronauts—both those who went into space and those who were on stand-by—who got a second life on the community speaker series circuit.

In a post-COVID world, perhaps the next iteration of the tent Chautauqua model is the modern TED talks. Dating to the early 1980s and premised on the same concept of bringing thinkers and lecturers to wide audiences, the modern TED talk relies on technology as the now-global access vehicle. Millions of people follow these programs, which now fully fulfill the original dream of the Chautauquas to bring educational programs to the masses. One can only imagine the kind of TED talk William Jennings Bryan could have delivered.

5

CAMP MEETINGS

S ome years ago, when we owned a summer cottage at the Mount Gretna Campmeeting, our neighbor would regale us with stories about community life in the old days. One afternoon, we got to talking about the Methodist church located in the camp meeting. Having grown up Presbyterian, attended Catholic schools and then married a Lutheran, I was naturally curious about the Methodist church. Our neighbor explained that the question was complex, as there were distinct differences of practice among the various Methodist churches, particularly in south-central Pennsylvania. That was an intriguing answer since, barring individual sermon styles, I assumed there would be no differences within the denomination. When pressed, our neighbor said that the Methodist church at Mount Gretna was very mainstream and thus pretty tame, in his opinion. His preference was to go to the Methodist religious service held a few miles down the road at the nearby Mount Lebanon Camp Meeting.

As he went on to explain, the Mount Lebanon congregation practiced "bloody Methodism." Well, that definitely intrigued me. He noted that bloody Methodist sermons were filled with talk of hellfire and damnation. They were evangelical and, in his words, reminiscent of southern tent revivals. He then went on to explain that both Mount Gretna and Mount Lebanon had histories connected to the Evangelical United Brethren (EUB) Church. The truly historic roots of that denomination stretch to the eighteenth century. Its more modern incarnation began with various small

Wesleyan Grove Camp Meeting 1845, Oak Bluffs, Mass.

This twentieth-century postcard depicts what a tent camp meeting would have looked like in the 1840s. In the center is a preaching platform with benches in front. Tents for sleeping were arranged in a semicircle behind.

denominational mergers starting in 1900. By the 1930s, it had coalesced into the new Evangelical United Brethren (EUB) denomination. Then in 1968, the Evangelical United Brethren merged with the Methodists to create the United Methodist Church. The story does not end as of this writing, as there is a new rift within the United Methodist Church over the issue of gay marriage that may result in a future schism. The Methodist story is complex, as it is for many denominations.

The EUB churches, while theologically close to the Methodists, were both socially conservative and highly evangelical in their services. As a result, in many south-central Pennsylvania towns, there was an unwritten understanding that there were moderate United Methodist churches, and then there were conservative EUB/Methodist churches. The church and camp meeting at Mount Gretna was of the moderate bent while Mount Lebanon represented the conservative or "bloody" Methodist strain.

How impactful was this? Well, today, every active camp meeting in the Mid-Atlantic region either is or was affiliated with the United Methodist Church. Recall as well that Chautauquas were born from the need for a place to train Methodist Sunday school teachers. Therefore, to understand the cottage communities is to begin with the story of Methodism.

The roots of the church can be traced to eighteenth-century England, where followers of John Wesley sought changes within the structure of the Episcopal Church. They built a doctrine around "new birth"—what some today might call being "born again." It was a visceral approach to religion that caught on with large numbers of people hungry for a personal religious experience. In a short time, they established a new denomination, calling themselves Methodists for the methodical way in which they carried out their Christian faith. At its heart, Methodism was a product of two immensely popular and widespread spiritual movements among English Protestants. The first was the First Great Awakening, which occurred roughly between 1730 and 1740 and led to the founding of the Methodist Church. It was followed fifty years later by the Second Great Awakening, which spanned from roughly 1790 to 1840. Theologically, this movement picked up where the first had left off and further built on that personal relationship with God in a new way. The Second Great Awakening galvanized many and gave rise to the modern fundamentalist religious movement. It also led to the creation of many camp meetings.

The camp meeting phenomenon began among the settlers in the rural portions of the United States along the spine of the Appalachian Mountains. Called the "back country" by historians, this was a region settled by British Isles and German settlers beginning in the mid-eighteenth century. Far from the large cities and centers of government, the backcountry was an area marked by an over-testosteroned sense of rugged individualism and self-determination. It was also a place where many English Protestant denominations adopted beliefs and methods of worship that made them distinctly American. A particular form of worship was the summer gathering of the faithful under a tent in the woods for revival services. The tent or grove camp meetings first appear, according to historian David Hackett Fischer in his landmark book *Albion's Seed*, among the backcountry Presbyterians. Within a short time, it spread to the Methodists and Baptists and became so popular that today, it is synonymous with Appalachian culture.

By the late 1700s, the Presbyterians were finding it increasingly difficult to provide ministers for their backcountry congregations. Their church required academically trained clergy, and as a result, the number of rural ministers was never as large as the need. Conversely, other denominations that were less strict in the formal education of clergy grew rapidly in the region. This was particularly true among the Methodists in the North and the Baptists in the South. As those denominations grew, fueled by

THE OUTDOOR CHAPEL, CENTRAL OAK HEIGHTS, WEST MILTON, PA.

This rustic open-air chapel continued to be used by many camp meetings, even after a tabernacle was constructed.

the fire of the Second Great Awakening, there was a rapid expansion of the number of camp meetings. By the 1830s, there were camp meetings throughout every part of the Mid-Atlantic region.

Much of central Pennsylvania (and this includes substantial parts of New York and Maryland) were settled by German Protestants. They came to colonial America from the region encompassing western Germany, eastern France and Switzerland. Originally invited to the region by William Penn, they were promised both Protestant religious freedom and economic opportunities. Thousands of people moved into the region, bringing a language and culture that was distinctly continental European. Theologically, these settlers covered the entire gamut of the Protestant spectrum, from Lutheran churches with elaborate liturgies to the Mennonites, who met in simple meetinghouses. The Reformation in Europe was arguably more complex than it was in Great Britain, with the result being that there were many schisms among the faithful that, in turn, gave birth to a wide range of smaller sects and splinter congregations. In America, it was that much worse, since the farther one was from a big city, the less control the large church denominations had over their congregation. Splits, splinters and theological fisticuffs were common and often resulted in the creation of new churches and denominations.

The simple message on the reverse of this 1912 postcard pithily highlighted the key elements of any successful camp meeting: "Meetings are good. Sinners Converted. Believers Sanctified. Preaching invited."

By the late 1830s, numerous camp meetings had been established throughout the backcountry. These camp meetings were held within a district consisting of several proximate church congregations. The district would identify a location, usually a centrally located farmer's field for the camp meeting. They would then determine the program and recruit guest preachers. Regional churches would help spread the word to families in the region. The services were grounded in evangelism, biblical study and hymn singing. At the heart of the camp meeting experience was the passion of the religious experience as shared by fellow believers even beyond the bounds of one's own denomination. As my dear friend Reverend Dr. Wayne Mell (retired, Presbyterian Church USA clergy) wrote to me in a June 2023 e-mail: "There was indeed a zeal for spreading the gospel and making converts at

In this 1986 photograph, a tent revival preacher in the American Southwest leads his congregation in prayer. The scene, with differences only in clothing styles, would have been identical in the 1700s, 1800s, 1900s and 2000s.

the heart of the Awakening, as well as privileging personal experience of the Spirit over strict adherence to denominational tradition and structures of authority. Indeed, much of the movement was characterized by cross-denominational organizing."

Tent or camp meetings were held in the summer months after planting and before the harvest. With summer, of course, came the dual risks of heat and thunderstorms, and the religious services were originally held in groves or stands of trees. Long sawbuck tables could be set up nearby for communal outdoor dining. For those who came a long distance and did not return home every day, small tents were made available for overnight accommodations. They were arranged around the central preaching tent or grove. John Cawman Eastlack kept a diary of his attendance at a tent camp meeting in 1866. His description offers a unique insight into the size of the community.

> *Today we are at the camp meeting. Of all the camps I have ever seen, this is the largest. 412 tents and still building more. The woods is literally full. One boarding house fed 1,000 for dinner. A better sermon than was preached this afternoon.*[12]

View of the Mammoth Tabernacle,
seating capacity 10,000, erected for the Rev. Billy Sunday's Revival Meetings,
McKeesport, Pa.

Billy Sunday was arguably the most famous evangelist in the early twentieth century. A former baseball player, Sunday had such a strong presence in the pulpit that people came from miles around to hear him preach. According to the caption, this building was constructed to accommodate ten thousand attendees to one of his services.

As camp meetings in groves became larger and more successful, the organizers would often procure a massive tent for the church services. Similarly, camp meeting associations were established, and they began constructing low wooden platforms for the tents. This had the advantage of getting participants off the ground in rainy weather as well as providing a physical delineation of camping spaces. Latrines and pumps followed as well to ensure safe water for everyone. The common tables made of logs, sawhorses and boards for eating were replaced with open-sided dining flyes and long metal tables.

Meal service came through a common kitchen operated by the camp meeting. Outside vendors also sold raw and prepared food. While they were seen as a source of additional revenue for the camp meetings, the food vendors also were also the source of internal disagreements. Camp meeting associations leased out to local merchants the privilege of selling goods. Our diarist, John Cawman Eastlack, kept the following account of the Centennial Camp Meeting Association's lease of rights to operate stands in the summer of 1869:

Cake and Bread stand to Andrew Turner for $355.00
Ice Cream Stand #1 to F.S. Parker for $360.00
Ice Cream Stand #2 to John Avis for $225
Hay and Feed stand to E.W. Bakley for $200
Meat Stand to Mr. Mattson for $35
Barber Shop to Charles Johnson for $12.50

The list not only shows what the scope of goods and services were but also provides where things were located. Clearly, Mr. Parker's ice cream stand was in a proximate location to the tabernacle and hence warranted a higher rental fee of $360 compared to Mr. Avis's "ice cream stand number two" that was rented for only $225.

Location, population and infrastructure limited the success of tent camp meetings. The property owner who leased the field, the thunderstorm that ruined the tents or a change in pastors could abruptly end a tent camp meeting. The Civil War was the biggest social disruptor of the nineteenth century. It affected camp meetings immensely. The loss of men to battle, disease and dismemberment put added pressure on returning and surviving farmers. Few families could afford to be away for tent revivals. By 1870, the old camp meeting movement was dead.

However, like the proverbial phoenix rising from the ashes, there was a new plan: the summer cottage camp meeting. This new model combined the older camp meeting religious experience with the addition of educational and recreational opportunities. Born from the effects of the industrial revolution and subsequent changes in the length of the workweek, middle-class families found themselves with the time and financial ability to go away for several weeks.

While having time to be away was significant, there was an even bigger change that popularized the cottage camp meeting. That change was the widespread advent of the railroad. By the third quarter of the nineteenth century, Americans in the Mid-Atlantic relied on the four great lines—the Pennsylvania, the Reading, the New York Central and the Baltimore and Ohio—to connect them within a day's journey to every great eastern city.

The diary of my great-uncle who lived in Pittsburgh chronicles more than one hundred train trips in just 1915. While some of the trips were done for his work in sales for the glass company, the majority were short trips to neighboring towns for lunch or dinner. Just as we run out for dinner if we cannot decide what to have, so did the middle class in the early 1900s—with a little more planning—using trains. After all, the inexpensive fares, regular schedule and incredible network of tracks meant that all of western Pennsylvania was accessible for an afternoon outing. Such a change was significant, as the older camp meetings were generally limited to local participants who arrived in buggies and wagons. The train meant guests could come from almost any city in the region to a camp meeting and still be home in time to sleep in their own beds. An example of this was the Chester Heights Camp Meeting located south of Philadelphia. Period accounts show that thousands of day-trippers came out from Philadelphia to attend services. So large were their numbers that the railroads added both extra cars and special trains to accommodate the guests. It was good money for the railroads and for the surrounding businesses, whether they employed hackney carriage drivers or local food merchants.

The Methodist Church saw the birth of a new camp meeting built around permanent cottages, proximate access to rail lines and summer recreation. These camps appealed to both summer residents and day visitors who came for a different set of experiences than the older camp meetings. All camp meeting communities share common elements. First, they have a tabernacle that was either a round or square building used for holding church services. Second, they have an arrangement of cottages constructed in either a rectangular grid of streets or like spokes emanating from the tabernacle. Camp meeting members usually owned only the cottage buildings themselves, while the denomination or camp meeting association owned and managed the land. Public infrastructure was the responsibility of the association. Public common outhouses and communal water pumps were first used, but then as the community prospered, public sewers, running water, electricity and paved roads were introduced.

Finding the right mix of recreation, religion and education was the biggest challenge for all the camp meetings. There were those who saw the community as existing for purely religious purposes and others who wanted a blend that included recreation and education. This boiled over into arguments about the serving of ice cream or the hours for curfews. Debates on these topics take up countless pages in the camp meeting histories of the modern era. The fights suggest that while most agreed on the overall purpose of camp meetings, all it took was one fox in the henhouse to start a melee about the merits of serving watermelon or allowing playground use on Sundays.

The successful camp meetings built their recreational programs around a lake, a stream or the ocean. While camp meetings often hoped to own their recreational bodies of water, it was usually the property of private or

The Rhodes Grove Tabernacle was a United Brethren Camp Meeting located near Chambersburg, Pennsylvania.

Davis and Mills were traveling evangelists who provided a program not unlike the tent Chautauquas to camp meetings. Well known in their era, they covered a territory stretching up and down the East Coast.

municipal interests. Public waterways, such as the Atlantic Ocean, were not as highly regulated as those that were privately owned. An example of the latter are the lakes at Pitman and Mount Gretna. For the owners, maximum revenue came from weekend use in the summer season. This caused friction when it came to Sunday operations. Still, the value of water to the cottage communities was immense. Most acknowledged the value of it for antsy children and odor control.

To address the needs of children, most camp meetings also constructed playgrounds. Located close to the tabernacle building, they were critical for burning off youthful energy and thus keeping parental sanity. While there were debates at some camp meetings about whether to allow playgrounds' use on Sundays, no one felt that they should be abolished. Today, those same playgrounds are still in use, albeit with bark mulch and fewer monkey bars.

The one great topic of debate for most of the camp meetings in the early twentieth century was access to Sunday newspapers. For my parents' generation, Sunday afternoons were devoted to reading the newspaper. It was considered by most to be a good, quiet activity on the day of rest. But there was a question about whether the delivery of said papers involved working on Sunday. Such was the division of views on this that a lawsuit was

TABERNACLE, CENTRAL OAK HEIGHTS, WEST MILTON. PA.

THIS AUDITORIUM SEATS 1,500 PERSONS   E-7455

Central Oak Heights Camp Meeting was so successful that the board of managers constructed this tabernacle, which was probably copied from a design by John Cilley. The shift into this building from its outdoor grove must have been an improvement on rain or hot days.

COTTAGES AT MARANATHA PARK - GREEN LANE, PA

Shrinking numbers of participants and rising land costs resulted in the closing of many camp meetings. The Pentecostal Marantha Camp Meeting in eastern Pennsylvania is a community that sadly no longer exists.

filed against Ocean View Camp Meeting's decision to prohibit the Sunday delivery of newspapers. While the suit failed and Sunday delivery occurred, it was one of those myriad touchpoints when modernity collided with the religious world.

The success or failure of cottage camp meetings was ultimately about the balancing act that each one made between past, present and future needs. This is not to say that the cottage camp meetings strayed from their religious purposes. There was an immutable norm for all of them that put religion at the center of their existence and decision-making. It was the small issues that niggled away at the core of the camp meetings and became destructive. Ultimately, finding the balance ensured that small camp meetings like Mount Lebanon, South Seaville and Brandywine Station have remained vibrant.

6

FROM OCEAN TO MOUNTAIN

Cottage Camp Meetings

T he cottage camp meetings were a unique subset of the much larger religious camp meeting movement. While there were probably several thousand tent and camp meetings in the eastern United States in the early twentieth century, there were perhaps fewer than five hundred with permanent cottages. The remainder were the more traditional tent meetings that met in a field for a week and then disappeared until the next season. So, how did a community shift from having tents to cottages?

In 1939, the Pennsylvania Conference of the United Brethren Church published a history of the denomination and provided a brief survey of the history of the camp meetings. It is a particularly insightful history, because the author notes that tent camp meetings had been established as a way for the denomination to test the waters in a region before establishing new churches. From an economic perspective, this made a great deal of sense, since the tent camp meetings were both highly evangelical in approach and relatively inexpensive to operate. If a local community flocked to attend a tent camp meeting, the denomination could consider establishing a new church in that area.

A majority of both the tent and cottage camp meetings did not last longer than a few decades. A lack of permanent infrastructure, including good rail access and a dearth of recreational opportunities, probably wiped out many of them after a few seasons. For those that became well established, there was an ongoing threat of natural disasters or national economic downturns such as the Great Depression. The 1939 history lists thirteen camp meetings, of which ten were reported in their annuals as having been closed. Two more were listed as being no longer affiliated with the denomination, and only one was still in existence. The year of the report is significant, since the Great Depression alone probably contributed to a significant number of closings. Today, several online resources list camp meetings primarily in the East. While these sources' accuracy is only as good as the information submitted to them, it appears that probably about one hundred cottage camp meetings remain in the Mid-Atlantic region.

Those that have survived to the present have done so because of a single factor: the deep familial ties that keep generations returning—or, to quote Tevye from *Fiddler on the Roof*, "It's tradition!" Betty Baver, a cottage owner at the Island Grove Camp Meeting in Mexico, Pennsylvania, described it this way:

> *We're old timers! My Grandmother Mertz owned the cottage, she gave it to my mother, my mother gave it to me. It was mostly my mother who took me. I was there as a kid.*[13]

The transfer of houses within families was clearly central to the success of every cottage community. Even today, camp meeting associations have far simpler rules for passing a cottage within a family than they do for selling to an outsider. Community is, after all, the heart of the camp meeting lifestyle.

One of the densest areas for camp meetings was southern and coastal New Jersey. This region was historically a hotbed for the camp meeting movement with a tradition that stretches back to the late 1700s. The cottage communities today are a product of the revival of the movement of the 1870s and 1880s. During that period, three distinct camp meetings evolved in the state. The first were mountain camp meetings located between Pennsylvania and New York. Second were those along the Atlantic Ocean, including the surviving communities of Ocean Grove, Island Heights and South Seaville. There were others, including such modern shore destinations as Asbury Park, Atlantic City and Cape May, that were born from this tradition. Secularism, however, triumphed over theology for many.

The third belt of camp meetings was located in southern New Jersey in a band stretching from Camden to Salem and then east toward the coast. This area was a hotbed of evangelical Methodism in the mid-nineteenth century that resulted in the founding of numerous camp meetings. Diarist John Cawman Eastlack wrote about attending a tent camp meeting in 1866 in Barnsboro (south of Camden), where ten thousand people attended services.

Today, the surviving camp meetings in this area include Malaga, one of the smallest, and Pitman, one of the largest.

The New Jersey camp meetings served attendees from throughout the Mid-Atlantic region. The communities in the north drew their visitors from the boroughs of New York. In the south, attendees came from Philadelphia and Wilmington.

OCEAN GROVE CAMP MEETING, NEW JERSEY

The largest of all the surviving cottage camp meetings, Ocean Grove remains a true anachronism along the New Jersey coast. Its creation was the result of the charismatic leadership of Reverend W.B. Osborn, a Methodist minister from Vineland, New Jersey, who set out to find a seaside location for a camp meeting. He wanted to find a spot on high ground with good water access and no mosquitos. The latter was a substantial problem that led to his vetoing Cape May as the home for his camp meeting.

Osborn's wife wrote a history of the community, in which she noted that God spoke to her husband and directed him to the location that became Ocean Grove. The good Lord was particularly wise that day, as the location was ideally situated fifty miles from New York City and ninety miles from Philadelphia. It had water on three sides to serve as a barrier for the outside world. The land was available for acquisition and seemed to have everything that was needed for a first-rate cottage community.

Osborn first visited the site in 1868, and one year later, he led a group of ministers and church leaders to obtain a charter from the New Jersey legislature to establish the Ocean Grove Camp Meeting Association of the Methodist Episcopal Church. Through various land acquisitions, the community soon expanded to comprise more than 260 acres.

Ocean Grove's successful growth over the succeeding decades was the result of both its perfect location and the thoughtful development of the community's infrastructure. Unlike camp meetings where residents owned their cottage building but not the land, Ocean Grove permitted approved members of the association to own their own property. Transportation, a vexing issue for all camp meetings, was carefully planned and resolved. Horse-drawn stages and, later, buses and automobiles provided access for those in nearby communities. The larger challenge was establishing rail service, as the closest line to the camp meeting stopped at nearby Long

OCEAN AVENUE FROM SOUTH END. OCEAN GROVE, N. J. 115

The beach is buzzing! This postcard shows a typical scene that could have been found along any beach in post–World War I America. The location, however, is the Ocean Grove Camp Meeting.

Branch. The camp meeting association recognized the need for direct rail service and purchased a substantial number of corporate bonds in the Farmingdale and New Egypt Railroad. The capital funding from those bonds enabled the railroad to extend its rail service to Ocean Grove. The investment was quite prudent, as the railroad generated more than $47,000 in revenue during its first year of expanded service.

There is a massive central tabernacle that accommodated several thousand people at the center. Smaller but no less elegant buildings flank the tabernacle and are still used for their original purpose of holding classes and meetings. A lawn or promenade extends from the tabernacle toward the ocean, providing a sweeping vista for people who are approaching.

A particularly striking aspect of the community is the ongoing use of personal tents resting on wooden platforms. This may be the last example of a cottage community continuing the nineteenth-century practice of having tented platforms for attendees. The platforms were the result of the problems that came from having tents rest on the damp, uneven and bug-infested ground. They not only made for a more comfortable experience for attendees but also formally defined spaces in the community that families came to feel were "theirs." Like the larger cottages, the platforms passed within families over the generations. By the mid-twentieth century,

In all camp meetings, the tabernacle is the spiritual and physical center of community programs and services.

Ocean Grove was and still is noted for its continued tradition of summer tent living.

small sheds abutted the platforms to provide privacy and storage. Today, these platform tents remain popular and are very personal spaces, with some residents colorfully decorating the tents and landscaping them.

Ocean Grove's success as a community was singularly predicated on its willingness to embrace recreation as a central component of the camp meeting experience. The authors of the 1944 *Diamond Jubilee History of Ocean Grove* make this point: "Ocean Grove was fast growing in popularity as a vacation spot, appealing especially to the religious element." Postcards from the early 1900s exclusively focus on the beach experience at Ocean Grove. To our modern eyes, the images are relatively banal, showing views of people playing in the water. But to a Methodist family looking to attend the camp meeting, they would have shown a spiritual and recreational nirvana.

Immediately north of Ocean Grove is Asbury Park, known to many through Bruce Springsteen's album *Greetings from Asbury Park*. The town was founded in 1871 and was named for the first bishop of the Methodist Episcopal Church. It grew up as a sister community to Ocean Grove with many of the same early restrictions. In the temperance era, covenants were added to property deeds that restricted the consumption of alcohol. However, things changed for Asbury Park, and the town became the very secular yin to the religious yang of Ocean Grove. A casino (defined in the nineteenth century as a public building for recreation) and a carousel were both constructed within one hundred yards of Ocean Grove. Alcohol consumption in bars became common. And with only a small body of water, some bridges and a few sand spits separating this wet town from Ocean Grove, one can only imagine the number of folks who slipped across the line for some medicinal spirits.

Ocean Grove, even as the largest of the camp meetings, struggles to ensure that its historic community values and traditions are preserved. It holds on to its Methodist heritage and pushes back on outside secular influences. In 2012, Superstorm Sandy destroyed the fishing pier owned by Ocean Grove. After the rubble was removed, plans were implemented to replace the pier with something more durable. When the design was announced, many outside the community were surprised to see that the pier was to be built in the shape of a giant cross. In the outside secular world, there was widespread pushback about whether a public pier should be constructed in the shape of a giant Christian cross. Ocean Grove reminded the outside world that it had a charter as a religiously based town, and thus, the choice of the pier's design was its decision alone. Despite some debates with the

State of New Jersey about construction details, the project proceeded and the pier opened in April 2023.

Ocean Grove is a true anachronism within the larger milieu of coastal resorts along the New Jersey coast. The *Diamond Jubilee History of Ocean Grove* devotes many pages to defending and debating Ocean Grove's distinctive community rules. These have changed over time, especially as state or federal laws have negated the association's rules. This was true on such hot-button issues as the Sunday train service or the personal consumption of alcohol. Private litigation challenged the blue laws regarding Sunday business and even the aforementioned local newspaper deliveries. Key to understanding these debates is the simple notion that Ocean View did not eschew modernity but rather simply wished to preserve the historical integrity of its community by limiting the impact of the outside world on it. Yet for all this, the community is also highly pragmatic in realizing that Atlantic Ocean is a significant draw for the public. A 1939 promotional history notes: "To all who owned property, this place resembled an important investment and cooperation between the governor and the governed was apparent."

SOUTH SEAVILLE CAMP MEETING, NEW JERSEY

While it is neither the largest nor the oldest camp meeting, South Seaville does enjoy the reputation of being the best preserved of all the early cottage camp meetings. The original plan developed by its founders was to construct a camp meeting at nearby Cape May. That area's abundance of flies drove the community inland, where it was founded in South Seaville in 1875.

The camp meeting's original community plan was laid out to allow for the construction of cottages on lots ranging from eighteen by thirty feet to forty by sixty feet. There was also land set aside to accommodate up to five hundred tents, although they disappeared as the number of cottages grew. The South Seaville plan is particularly distinctive because of its extensive focus on green spaces interspersed among the cottages. At the center was Wesley Park, with an open tabernacle and pulpit. Cottage lots were arranged geometrically outward from the tabernacle and around four distinctive parks: Embury, George, Asbury and Cook Parks. While cottage communities often had such open green spaces, the park system in South Seaville was far more elaborate. The community set down rules about keeping horses out of the park and noted that certain parks were just for men and others were only for women.

The gable end of the South Seaville Tabernacle is one of the most striking elements of the entire community. It remains remarkably unchanged.

The community plan at South Seaville is among the best documented for all the cottage communities. These plans included detailed instructions about the proximity of the cottages to the tabernacle and even made a provision of a cottage for visiting clergy. There was also a large boardinghouse to accommodate single individuals and small families. A laundry, store, firehouse, garage and public shower area were all set out as well. Common among many camp meetings was a children's tabernacle, built to house youth classes and programs. Of particular interest was the construction in 1887 of an ice cream parlor. It proved so successful that it closed only when a modern ice cream freezer was installed in the general store during the 1950s. Various services, including a barber, a professional photographer and a hackney service to transport people to the train, were also available. As for recreation, the community had a children's playground but lacked any large water feature like a lake. The nearby beach resorts were already a big draw for summer vacations, so bus services were arranged to take camp meeting members to nearby beaches.

South Seaville is probably the most intact of all the Victorian-era cottage communities in the Mid-Atlantic. Many of the houses retain their original footprint, and the structure of the parks and various buildings is easy to follow. Still following the camp meeting's religious mission, ownership of the houses requires membership in the camp meeting association.

WEST JERSEY GROVE CAMP MEETING/MALAGA CAMP MEETING ASSOCIATION, NEW JERSEY

Founded in 1873 as the West Jersey Camp Meeting by the Methodist Church, Malaga was constructed around a massive man-made lake that provided built-in recreational opportunities for residents. The community originally had more than one hundred cottages, although its present number is far less.

Malaga is arranged in a rectangular grid with a cinder block–constructed tabernacle located in the center. The cottages range from two-story Victorian examples to the more abundant one-story cottages of the early twentieth century. Of particular interest is the small chapel, an uncommon feature of camp meetings. The larger tabernacle was generally used for most services.

Malaga's success is a result of the numerous families who continue to pass its cottages on to succeeding generations. With the demise of lake swimming, the construction of a swimming pool has helped the community modernize its recreational offerings. The community still operates as a camp meeting.

One can only guess the reason why so many of the West Jersey Grove Camp Meeting residents came outside their cottages in August 1912 for this photograph. Perhaps there was a Sunday school event.

PITMAN CAMP MEETING, NEW JERSEY

The incorporated borough and former camp meeting of Pitman was named for Charles Pitman, a highly charismatic Methodist elder who spoke at numerous revivals in the 1820s. He was said to have been singularly able to keep an audience captivated by one of his sermons for more than two hours. Pitman's success can be summarized in two words that are found in early community descriptions: "convenient and desirable." Located within a very short distance of Camden and Philadelphia, Pitman was the largest and most accessible of all the camp meetings in the southern region. Interestingly, Pitman and Ocean Grove share a common history and development. Both have deep roots in the Methodist cottage camp meeting movement of the post–Civil War period and share several founders/leaders and members.

Pitman was established in 1871 using a plan that called for the cottage sites to be leased rather than sold to residents. The center of the original fourteen-acre camp meeting was a wooden tabernacle. Radiating outward in the shape of a wagon wheel were twelve small streets. The number twelve was significant, as it represented the number of apostles. The first cottages were located in the center of the hub, and as the community grew,

Pitman was one of the largest camp meetings in the Mid-Atlantic.

the buildings expanded geometrically outward. The larger cottages were constructed farther out on a rectangular grid system that was laid out to accommodate the larger parcels.

The hub at Pitman is noteworthy, as it is among the few of this design left in America. It was derived from the older pre-1850 circular tent camp meeting model. What worked for tents did not for buildings. As one drew closer to the center of the hub, housing lots got smaller, and the orientation of the front door became challenging. The hub was also a logistical challenge for the delivery and parking of both wagons and automobiles. Yet the charm of walking along one of the spokes with the tabernacle at the visual and metaphoric heart of the community remains obvious.

The key to Pitman's long success was its extensive and reliable regional rail service. As it was a "modern camp meeting," high prominence was given to the location of the railroad lines that brought attendees, speakers and provisions to the town. By 1878, there were 6 trains per day going from Camden to Pitman. Fast-forward to 1926, when that numbered increased to 25 trains per day, the fastest of which made the trip to Camden in just twenty-seven minutes. While the train service was the topic of both admiration and envy by other communities, there were

FIRST AVENUE, PITMAN, N.J.

First Avenue is one of the twelve streets that, like spokes on a wheel, radiated outward from the tabernacle in Pitman. As the oldest part of the community, the cottages are very densely sited on their lots.

problems. Like its other modern cousin Ocean Grove, Pitman had a long and contentious fight about allowing Sunday rail service. For the most devout in the community, Sundays were times for total quiet and spiritual contemplation. Thus, the hustle, bustle, smoke and sound of passenger trains were disruptive and must be prohibited. A challenge to that notion came from day visitors and weeklong guests who were completely reliant on the Sunday rail service to get home. The railroad companies had to walk the metaphorical tightrope between customer and church demands. Initially, the solution was to have all Sunday train service stop in a nearby town. Of course, this meant that those Sunday travelers had to extra time and expense to get to and from Pitman. A carriage would then be arranged to pick up guests in the nearby town and bring them to Pitman. The process was then reversed when residents left at the end of a stay. So great was this need for carriages to a nearby town that on August 11, 1889, an estimated 1,400 carriages made the trip to and from Pitman.

While the camp meeting association was dealing with the Sunday train issues, there was a new threat to the camp meeting. By the 1890s, train travel was so easy that urban families began to consider living in the new "suburbs." These new suburbanites quickly recognized Pitman's existing and exceptional rail service, and year-round houses were soon built for their use. With this influx of year-round residents, the camp meeting came under new pressures to deal with the Sunday train issue. In 1904, Sunday train service was implemented when the camp meeting was not in session. Two years later, the walls fell, and the trains were allowed to stop in town on Sundays during the camp meeting season.

Another reason for Pitman's success was its proximity to neighboring Alcyon Park and its lake. Founded in 1892, the park was to be named Halcyon, derived from the ancient Greek word for "idyllic." However, the park's founder felt that too many people would mispronounce the word and dropped the "H." The park had everything from boardwalks and swimming areas to a carousel, bowling alleys, a roller-skating rink, a toboggan slide and a movie theater. What the Atlantic Ocean was to Ocean Grove, so Alcyon Park was to Pitman. Families from southern New Jersey, particularly Camden, flocked to the park in the summer.

One interesting aspect of Alcyon Park was its owners' creation of a summer spectacle event. They decided that to draw a new audience, they would re-create a historical event on the lake, complete with fireworks. It was to be a spectacle on a grand scale. In the summer of 1905, Alcyon Lake was home to a mock Battle of Port Arthur, based on the recently finished Russo-

Alcyon Park abutted Pitman Camp Meeting and provided much-needed recreation for attendees. It was also popular with day trippers from the nearby Camden.

Japanese War. The media reported that more than two thousand rockets were set off, leading to the total destruction of the model Russian fleet. It was also reported more than ten thousand people came to watch the "battle." Assuming that each person purchased a ticket, there was clearly big money in the spectacle. Events like this were not unique to Alcyon. Harrisburg, the state capital of Pennsylvania, in 1889 and for several years after, re-created the explosion of Mount Vesuvius, complete with ash and lava. These events were big financial wins not only for the promoter but also for the surrounding community's merchants. There is no doubt that some in the camp meeting were not happy about the noise and influx of spectators, but the boon for the merchants tempered their concerns.

By the mid-twentieth century, the commuter residents dominated the town's population, leaving the camp meeting association more and more isolated. Public policy disputes with the camp meeting association often resulted in lawsuits. The power of the camp meeting was waning. By 1970, the camp meeting association closed, and it sold its remaining assets to the Borough of Pitman. It was a prudent move, as its costs to operate far exceeded its revenue from the dwindling membership rolls. The risk, of course, was that in dissolving the camp meeting, local real estate speculators would step in and bulldoze the community. The 1970s was a challenging period for the town's urban planning, and it was often common to see older buildings destroyed in favor of parking lots and strip malls. This appeared to be the fate for Pitman's historic camp meeting. Thankfully, the plans to bulldoze the camp meeting for parking lots were shelved, and the core of the historic area remains. While it is now a year-round residential community, Pitman retains much of the character of the old camp meeting.

Pennsylvania Camp Meetings

Pennsylvania camp meetings followed a similar pattern of development to those in New Jersey. Most were established by the Methodist Church or the Evangelical United Brethren around a lake or stream. The camp meetings were generally located in three large belts. The first were those founded around the perimeter of Philadelphia. They flourished thanks to the train service that brought Methodists out from the city to the country. The second group of camp meetings runs west from Delaware County along the southern border of the state. This area was a hotbed of Methodism, with participants coming from Wilmington, Baltimore and the regional cities of York, Harrisburg and Chambersburg. The third belt of camp meetings went west from Lancaster County and then north along the Susquehanna River. The majority of these were run by the United Brethren and Evangelical United Brethren Churches.

Mount Lebanon Camp Meeting, Pennsylvania

Mount Lebanon was established by the ancestor denominations of the Evangelical United Brethren Church and is currently affiliated with the United Methodist Church. It is located just north of the city of Lebanon in Lebanon County. The community is among the best preserved of the larger camp meetings in Pennsylvania, with a significant number of original structures still standing today.

Founded in 1892, the camp meeting's location was convenient to a number of small towns in the Lebanon Valley, including Lebanon, Annville, Cleona and Palmyra. The community also heavily benefited from the nearby trolley system that was put into place by local chocolatier Milton Hershey to transport workers to his factories in nearby Hershey. Mount Lebanon was established as a tent camp meeting, but cottages followed within a year of its founding. In fact, the cottages appeared so quickly that the camp meeting association had to establish a Committee on the Erection of Cottages. Their task was to establish and then enforce rules for cottage construction. The rules noted that all the cottages had to be both completely whitewashed and two stories tall. By 1900, there were thirty-three cottages and one hundred tents in the camp meeting.

Of particular importance at Mount Lebanon is the tabernacle, which was erected by local engineer John Cilley, who also designed and oversaw the construction of both the tabernacle and the auditorium at the Mount Gretna Campmeeting and the Pennsylvania Chautauqua, respectively. Cilley's system of structural cabling to support the roof framing ensured that there were only a limited number of added uprights needed. This, in turn, ensured that most people could enjoy an unobstructed view of the pulpit during services.

Mount Lebanon had the reputation of being far more evangelical than most camp meetings. There are stories—perhaps apocryphal in origin—that say the Sunday services began at 7:00 a.m. and ran without interruption until 9:00 p.m. There were also legendary preachers who became so enraptured with their sermons that during the service, they had to clutch trees and posts to keep themselves upright.

Food was always a critical part of all the cottage communities, and Mount Lebanon was no exception. The association leased kitchen operations to local vendors. They also completed a regular schedule of kitchen upgrades over the subsequent decades, including the daring move in 1900 to seasonally rent a modern cooking range for the sum of twelve dollars. The need was obvious, as in one previous season, it was reported that the kitchen served more than five thousand people on a single weekend.

The subject of camp meeting food was apparently very complicated. While most had their own kitchens, there was a booming local concession service that allowed outside vendors to sell food. For example, at the Island Grove Camp Meeting in Mexico, Pennsylvania, the local Amish community sold baked goods during the summer. So lucrative was this deal for the vendors that at Pitman, an irate vendor rammed the camp meeting gates because he was not granted one of the association's limited selling licenses. Mount Lebanon had its share of troubles without outside vendors, and often, it was a matter of theology rather than gastronomy. In 1910, the camp meeting association banned the Sunday sale of ice cream and bananas. One can only imagine the debates on how sinfully good a banana was on a Sunday.

By the 1950s, Mount Lebanon had built a reputation for its Pennsylvania Dutch fare. Today, we would call this the kind of country cooking that involves a lot of sugar, lard, potatoes and pork. As good as this food was, however, it did not stop an investigation by the state board of health, which noted that the restaurant needed to put in window screens to keep out the flies.

Mount Lebanon remains a remarkably intact example of an early twentieth-century camp meeting. It has survived, ironically, through the actions of the state government. The Pennsylvania Department of Environmental Resources claimed that it had only recently discovered the existence of the community in 1989. As such, it issued regulations for the ratio of purely summer cottages versus year-round residents. The purpose of these restrictions, despite sounding arbitrary and capricious, was, in fact, to prevent over-taxing utility services, road and parking issues and other infrastructure upgrades that the camp meeting could not afford. As a result, Mount Lebanon retains both its architectural presence and community identity.

Mount Gretna Campmeeting

The Mount Gretna Campmeeting (officially written as one word) is an interesting part of the overall narrative of Robert Coleman's dream for Mount Gretna that consisted of a public recreational park, the home of the Pennsylvania Chautauqua and the mustering fields for the Pennsylvania National Guard. The story begins with the Stoverdale Camp Meeting, located along the banks of the Swatara Creek, midway between the towns of Middletown and Hummelstown just outside of Hershey, Pennsylvania. The camp meeting was established there because of the area's location along a bucolic creek and its stop for the Hummelstown-Brownstone Railroad (HBR). The HBR provided rail service from the nearby brownstone quarries to the Pennsylvania Railroad Company's main lines. While it was mostly a tent camp meeting with some cottages, Stoverdale was relatively quiet until 1891, when things suddenly took a turn for the worse. A disagreement among the camp meeting's membership and the association board resulted in a schism.

Then entered Robert Coleman, who offered land to one of the parties at his new community of Mount Gretna. For Coleman, the new camp meeting meant both new revenues and a stable summer clientele. In 1892, a delegation of former Stoverdale Camp Meeting Association members arrived in Mount Gretna to look at real estate options. What followed was

A Romantic Spot along the Swatara, near Middletown, Pa.

This postcard shows part of the Stoverdale Camp Meeting near Hummelstown, Pennsylvania. A schism within the community led to the founding of the Mount Gretna Campmeeting.

the establishment of the Mount Gretna Campmeeting Association and a subsequent agreement with Robert Coleman to purchase a significant tract of land for the community. The new camp meeting property was laid out using a rectangular grid with a central tabernacle. John Cilley was brought in to design this structure while also working on the auditorium at the Chautauqua. Tree-lined common park areas surrounded the community, and there were walls, fencing and gates to control access to the community.

Set on a hillside, the cottage lots varied in size, with the smallest being closest to the tabernacle and the larger ones being more openly spaced farther up the hill behind the community. Approximately one hundred cottages were constructed in the first year, the majority completed before 1910. Despite such a narrow window of construction, there is a remarkably diverse range of architectural styles found in the camp meeting. Rubbing shoulder in Mount Gretna Campmeeting are Adirondack bungalows, Shingle Style houses and even the odd late Gothic cottage.

There has been a long-told narrative among camp meeting residents that a majority of the present cottages began life as tents that were then followed by platforms with tents on top. The platforms were enclosed, creating ground-level cottages. Finally, as residents wanted more prestige

Otterbein Lodge   Camp Meeting Grounds   Street Scene
Mt. Gretna, Penna.

Tabernacle   Chapel

A 1958 postcard of the camp meeting grounds at Mount Gretna.

in the community, the ground-level cottages were elevated and enlarged, leading to the construction of high porches, where families could look down on their neighbors.

This story speaks volumes about the families in the community and how they wished to be perceived. However, the story itself is apocryphal, with little basis in facts. The original community plan did not include a set-aside area for tents or platforms, as one sees in other cottage communities. While there are surviving images that show tents, they do not appear to have lasted very long.

Mount Gretna's cottages were built onto a rocky hillside, with most resting on elevated piers to ensure a level floorplan. As a result, many are between one and three feet above the ground. In this case, the elevated porches were not about class as much as they were about the physical leveling of the house.

The Mount Gretna Campmeeting Association, like its cousin at Ocean Grove, struggled with the influence of surrounding secularization. Sunday, as the Sabbath, was a day of rest, and camp meetings generally shut down all work, including retail and train travel. Mount Gretna closed and locked its gates on Sundays to provide quiet calm for residents. That said, there are

Chautauqua Gate to the Camp Meeting Grounds, Mt. Gretna, Pa.

This unusual postcard shows the ticket collector at the entrance to the Mount Gretna Campmeeting. Managed access provided both safety and revenue for the community.

Where days are delightful, Mount Gretna, Pa.

John Cilley designed the camp meeting tabernacle as well as the auditorium in the adjacent Chautauqua.

A cottage at Chester Heights Camp Meeting. *Photograph by Jane S. Seibert.*

A cottage ready for summer guests. *Photograph by Jane S. Seibert.*

The tabernacle at Chester Heights Camp Meeting. *Photograph by Jane S. Seibert.*

A garden Buddha at Mount Gretna. *Photograph by Jane S. Seibert.*

Looking through a window. *Photograph by Jane S. Seibert.*

A cottage at Chester Heights Camp Meeting. *Photograph by Jane S. Seibert.*

A well-maintained Shingle Style cottage at Mount Gretna. *Photograph by Jane S. Seibert.*

An Adirondack-style cottage at Mount Gretna. *Photograph by Jane S. Seibert.*

One of the largest Mount Gretna cottages, complete with its own ballroom. *Photograph by Jane S. Seibert.*

Left: Getting ready for autumn with a stack of firewood by the cottage. *Photograph by Jane S. Seibert.*

Below: A classic cottage painted in white. *Photograph by Jane S. Seibert.*

Three different exterior paint schemes at Landisville Camp Meeting. *Photograph by Jane S. Seibert.*

Porches as outdoor rooms on a cottage. *Photograph by Jane S. Seibert.*

Wonderful architectural details abound on many cottages. *Photograph by Jane S. Seibert.*

Boston ferns in hanging baskets are a near-universal element. *Photograph by Jane S. Seibert.*

Foundation plantings provide both privacy screening and shade for the porch, and they add color and visual interest to the exterior. *Photograph by Jane S. Seibert.*

The owners of this cottage carefully blend exterior plantings and paint choices to create a harmonious appearance, all guarded by a modern green man. *Photograph by Jane S. Seibert.*

Geraniums and calendulas add a splash of bright color to the corner of this cottage. *Photograph by Jane S. Seibert.*

The never-ending saga of roof maintenance at a cottage. *Photograph by Jane S. Seibert.*

"Vinyl-cide" cover original decorative wooden elements with modern vinyl siding. *Photograph by Jane S. Seibert.*

Entering Pitman Camp Meeting. *Photograph by Jane S. Seibert.*

The Hall of Philosophy, Pennsylvania Chautauqua at Mount Gretna. *Photograph by Jane S. Seibert.*

A modern adaptation of a former CLSC building. *Photograph by Jane S. Seibert.*

John Cilley designed the tabernacle at Mount Gretna Camp Meeting. *Photograph by Jane S. Seibert.*

Cilley also designed the auditorium at the Pennsylvania Chautauqua at Mount Gretna. Today, it is home to Gretna Theater. *Photograph by Jane S. Seibert.*

The tabernacle, Landisville Camp Meeting. *Photograph by Jane S. Seibert.*

The tabernacle's interior, Landisville Camp Meeting. *Photograph by Jane S. Seibert.*

Painted Lady Cottage at Chester Heights Camp Meeting. *Photograph by Jane S. Seibert.*

An amazing exterior color scheme at Chester Heights Camp Meeting. *Photograph by Jane S. Seibert.*

The famous Jigger Shop Ice Cream Parlor at Mount Gretna. So many calories and so little time! *Photograph by Jane S. Seibert.*

stories about residents slipping over the fence to obtain fresh-baked goods from a nearby shop on Sunday mornings.

Like most cottage communities, Mount Gretna evolved over the decades to account for the changing world around it. A permanent Methodist church building was constructed to provide ministery to year-round residents. With it came a large parking lot in the heart of the community that was welcomed by those who were tired of carrying groceries to their cottage on cold, rainy February days.

The community also shifted toward a more secular approach to cottage ownership. By the time I purchased my cottage in the early 2000s, there was still a formal application process for residency that asked about church affiliation. My former wife had been raised Methodist, so this easily solved any issues. We were required to meet with the camp meeting representatives, who let us know the rules about leaf and trash removal, as well as when work on the cottage was permitted. Our house, modified for year-round use some years prior, was nicknamed the "divorcée's cottage." This appellation was rooted in an important change in the demographic of the community that began in the 1970s. As cottages were weatherized

Otterbein Ave., Campmeeting
Grounds, Mt. Gretna, Pa.

25-1

Notice the three different types of second-floor window treatments. The most elegant was the full porch on the first house followed by the glassed-in forebay on the second house and the simple outside walkway on the third. All were probably used as sleeping porches.

for year-round use, they became popular with newly divorced singles who wanted smaller digs that were also readily affordable. The result was a regular rotation of buyers who acquired the house during divorce and then sold it when they remarried.

Outside of the divorcées, the other camp meeting residents were retirees who moved there to enjoy the area's cultural opportunities. The programs in the camp meeting and at the nearby Chautauqua covered everything from art classes and nature walks to, of course, biblical study. One highlight of the season was the Black Eagle Jazz Band, which performed annually in the camp meeting as part of a special jazz church service that attracted standing room–only crowds. The community's quality of life was wonderful, particularly for retirees. Things were not all roses, however, as changes have continued to press in on the community.

Mount Gretna Campmeeting is now a community that has successfully threaded the needle of moving from the past to the future without the pain and anguish other camp meetings have encountered. Even in its modern secularism, Mount Gretna remains a community that is very sensitive to its collective history.

Herndon Camp Meeting

When I was a boy, my family would travel from Harrisburg, north to the town of Milton, Pennsylvania, where my grandmother had been born. The trip, to a young boy, was a pretty boring mix of farmers' fields and small towns. The one highlight was going through the town of Herndon, located on the eastern side of the Susquehanna River. It represented to both my head and stomach a median point between our house and lunch.

Herndon is a small community that touches the Mahantango Valley, an area identified by scholars as a center of traditional Pennsylvania German culture. Here, the Pennsylvania Dutch dialect is still spoken by many, and New Year's Day dining is always about pork and sauerkraut. The German evangelical denominations were particularly strong in the community, and thus, it was not surprising that, in 1874, a tent camp meeting was established in a local farmer's field. For the next twenty-six years, the camp meeting moved from field to field, depending on the farmer's rotation of crops. By 1901, the association decided it needed to obtain a permanent location, complete with cottages. They issued stock to raise the capital needed to purchase the land.

HERNDON CAMPMEETING   SOUTH EAST CORNER

When they were originally built, the Herndon Camp Meeting cottages were all probably identical. Over time, as families personalized them, the houses gained shutters, dormers, screened porches, balconies and other elements.

A history of the camp meeting, written in 1910, notes that there were thirty-one cottages, a boardinghouse and numerous tents. While cottages could be built, tents were readily available to rent for $2.50. If one wanted a tent resting on a wooden platform, the rent jumped to $3. If a family had many children, wooden bunks were available for $1 each, and straw for the floor could be procured for $0.10 per tent. Breakfast cost $0.25, and dinner cost $0.35, with children under five eating for free. It was quite the enterprise in free markets.

This same community history lists all the cottage owners and their hometowns. Six intrepid souls were from the town of Herndon, located less than a mile away. Of the remaining twenty-five owners, nine were from towns within ten miles of Herndon, and fifteen were from Pennsylvania towns about half a day away by train. The odd member was Mrs. A.J. McKinney, who hailed from Spokane, Washington. She was probably a former Herndon native who had moved west and came back every year. It is not surprising that so many attendees came from homes within an hour of the camp meeting. Camp meetings were built on the concept of creating a short-term community of believers. Thus, even coming from less than a mile away was not as important as it was to be seen gathering with your fellow church members at the camp meeting.

Brandywine Summit Camp Meeting

Located just north of the Delaware state line in southern Delaware County, Brandywine Station is a lone survivor of what had once been numerous nineteenth-century cottage camp meetings located in the townships surrounding Philadelphia. Urban development has since resulted in the loss of most camp meetings, but Brandywine Summit has remained. The camp meeting association was chartered in 1884 and soon thereafter entered a lease to rent its site. In 1943, the community secured the funding to purchase that site. The tabernacle is believed to date from 1884, with the majority of its sixty-six cottages dating from the early twentieth century. The cottages all comprise one story, as stipulated by the association's by-laws.

The camp meeting was laid out around two common areas. The first was the tabernacle with surrounding cottages. The second currently opens to the parking area and has a central picnic grove that is flanked by cottages on three sides. Brandywine Summit is unique in that several properties of its owners have purchased adjacent cottages and connected them to create larger houses.

When preparing for this book, I happened to visit this community just prior to Sunday afternoon service. Walking among the cottages and trees, I heard the bell by the tabernacle ring. The doors opened on the cottages, and out came the residents, walking toward the tabernacle as their families have done for nearly a century. It was a magical moment that could have occurred in 2023, 1923 or 1893.

Chester Heights Camp Meeting

Visiting Chester Heights Camp Meeting is challenging today. This camp meeting was established as the Philadelphia Camp Meeting and Excursion Society under the control of the Methodist Episcopal Church. Chartered in 1870, it secured a site on a farm in Logtown, now the town of Chester Heights in southern Chester County. The camp meeting flourished because of its excellent rail service to Philadelphia via the Pennsylvania Railroad. According to the community's history, the trains brought upward of four thousand day attendees during the peak of the camp meeting's season.

The cottages were built in a loose circle around the central tabernacle at the crest of a hill. The community expanded down the hillside, with additional cottages located on various levels as one moved toward the stream at the bottom of the hill. Unfortunately, a series of fires and a destructive windstorm reduced the community's number of cottages from the three hundred (reported in 1988) to less than twenty-four today. Portions of the original expansive tract have been carved away for urban development, resulting in the loss of the rural character. Yet the community is not lost. Work has recently been undertaken to renovate the original dormitory building to make way for a modern conference center. Some of the cottages are attractive and simply wanting for residents, while others are in various states of disrepair. The future of the community seems precarious, and I suspect it could easily disappear in the next decade.

Penn Grove Camp Meeting and Summit Grove Camp Meeting

Both of these camp meetings are located in southern York County in the heart of what has been described as the Pennsylvania Bible Belt. Penn Grove was founded in 1898 and lasted as a camp meeting until the 1960s, when it fell into disuse. Summit Grove opened in 1865, although most of its buildings date to the 1890s. Summit Grove was acquired by the Christian and Missionary Alliance denomination in 1936; it then, in turn, repurposed

The Penn Grove Camp Meeting relied more on the "apartment" block model for residences. This style of building was more common in the South than it was in the Mid-Atlantic.

HOTEL, SUMMIT GROVE CAMP, NEW FREEDOM, PA.

Even the smallest of camp meetings often had a hotel for use by singles, couples or visiting clergy.

the community as a nondenominational conference center in 2000. Both Summit Grove and Penn Grove were similar in structure, with a central tabernacle that was surrounded by two-story cottages.

Both camp meetings rose and ultimately fell as a result of the growth and then collapse of the local railroad service. The southern York region has stronger cultural and business ties to Baltimore than to Philadelphia or Harrisburg. As such, the residents of Baltimore could have easily take a train from the city and north into Pennsylvania to attend a camp meeting. Add to this a large Evangelical United Church population in the region, and the communities had a formula for success. With the advent of the automobile, travel to the camp meetings by train decreased, and soon, the railroads cut service. Unable to attract large numbers of Baltimoreans, the communities declined. A lack of a large lake or another recreational feature did not help, and by the 1960s, both were in steep decline.

Juniata Valley Camp Meeting and Island Grove Camp Meeting

These two camp meetings are located in north-central Pennsylvania. The Juniata Valley Camp Meeting was also known as the Newton Hamilton

Camp Meeting. Founded in 1872, its residences differ dramatically from those of the other Pennsylvania camp meetings. Residents used long, two-story side-by-side apartment or townhouse blocks. When they were opened, horizontal flaps attached to the exterior walls allowed for light and air circulation. These long buildings with wooden side flaps are common in both southern and Appalachian camp meetings but not in Pennsylvania.

Island Grove Camp Meeting is located along the banks of the Juniata River. The community was established by the Evangelical United Brethren and served the local community. The cottages are two-story-tall Gothic Revival cottages, much like those in South Seaville, but they are now lacking in much of their original architectural detail. Sadly, flooding along the Juniata River has damaged and destroyed many of the community's original houses. It remains in operation.

7

SPIRITUALIST CAMPS

Many years ago, I mounted a museum exhibition on the photographer who worked at Camp Silver Belle, a spiritualist camp located in Ephrata, Lancaster County. The exhibit attracted a lot of attention, and I was frequently invited to speak about the history of spiritualism, the camp and its photographer. In doing my research, I discovered a fascinating historical narrative that spanned the centuries and included such notables as Mary Todd Lincoln, Harry Houdini and Arthur Conan Doyle.

The story of spiritualism begins on the eve of the American Revolution with two great writers: Thomas Paine and Benjamin Franklin. Both espoused a doctrine known as Deism, based on the notion that the divine had set the universe in motion but then never interfered again in man's affairs. Deism did not just rock the eighteenth-century theological boat—it darned nearly sank it. Deism's followers promoted a broad definition of free will, insofar as God was seen more as a passive bystander to humankind's actions on Earth. Direct involvement by God was gone, and humanity, it could be argued, was truly not at the center of the universe.

While popular in its day, Deism came to be regarded as a spiritually cold doctrine, as it offered little hope for eternal salvation. The great machine that ran it all did not take into account the actions, good or bad, of individuals, so atonement and redemption had no purpose. Even the most theologically jaded individuals had a hard time accepting humanity as just a sidebar in the universe.

The pushback on Deism was manifested by the fervor of the Second Great Awakening. The nineteenth-century theologians behind that movement rejected the concept of a great machine-operated universe and instead advocated that to have a personal relationship with the divine was critical. God's presence was manifest in the world, and the path between heaven and Earth was permeable. That fundamental shift opened a spiritual door by allowing the dead to return to Earth to help the living. Thus, crossover communication could occur based on the simple notion that God and the angels could communicate directly with humans in order to help them. Vastly different than the mathematical creator espoused in Deism, this new definition of God was of a kind and caring figure who used his powers and those of his angels to physically help humanity.

Death is, of course, the greatest of all mysteries. It is witnessed by all but reported by none. Tragic death, when it comes to the young or through an accident or war, is particularly difficult for survivors to comprehend. In the nineteenth century, the art of modern warfare, the power of technology and the rise of industrialism lead to more tragic death than had been experienced in any other period. The most visible and symbolic of such deaths was the highly public loss of Prince Albert, the husband of Queen Victoria, who died of illness at the age of forty-two. In such grief at the loss, the queen entered a formal period of mourning that lasted forty years. In a much-publicized painting of Queen Victoria's 1887 jubilee celebration, the artist depicts an elderly Victoria seated alone in a black mourning dress, sometimes called widow's weeds. She is surrounded by dozens of colorfully bedecked soldiers, princes and court ladies. The contrast was deliberate and highlighted the then-decades-long mourning she felt for her husband. Then, as now, what the royal family did was copied and emulated by the public on a grand scale. The result of Victoria's public mourning was a cottage industry around death that began with manner books. Written by socialites and clergy, these books provided detailed instructions on how and when to mourn. Thus, the death of a parent would entail a black armband for a man or black dress for a woman, and it would be worn for twelve months; meanwhile, the same band would be worn for only forty days for a cousin or uncle.

The subject of mourning hit home during and immediately following the Civil War. Identification discs (or dog tags as they were called in later wars) were not issued in the Civil War, nor was there a good system of accounting for the bodies of soldiers following large or complex engagements. As a result, many families never heard a word about what happened to their loved

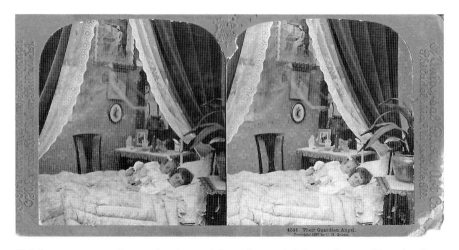

This fantasy stereocard was to be observed through a special viewer that would render the scene three dimensionally. In the nineteenth century, when this card was made, there was a widespread belief in the manifestation of angels in the world.

one, nor was there any opportunity to mark or visit a grave. It left questions unanswered and spiritual wounds gaping for a generation of Americans.

Because of this fascination with death and the afterlife, a host of talented writers produced a range of fictional accounts about the boundaries between life and death. One includes in this dark anthology nineteenth-century authors Edgar Allan Poe (*The Raven*, etc.), Mary Shelley (*Frankenstein*), Robert Louis Stevenson (*Dr. Jekyll and Mr. Hyde*) and Bram Stoker (*Dracula*). *Dracula* and *Frankenstein* in particular tread on the fundamental question of whether life can come from death. While all these works are considered classic examples of the Gothic genre today, the era's most famous book about the afterlife focuses on a holiday story.

Charles Dickens's *A Christmas Carol* is fundamentally about the power of spirits—in this case, the ghosts of Christmas past, present and future. Each appears in the span of just one night to visit and then save the troubled and morally bankrupt Ebenezer Scrooge. While these three ghosts are unknown to Scrooge, the story begins with a visit from a ghost he does know, that of his former business partner and friend Jacob Marley. Marley can no longer save himself, but he can save Scrooge. The end, as we all know, is Scrooge becoming self-aware of who he had become and vowing to change. The ghosts are presumed to be satisfied with the result and consider their work accomplished. Eliminating the familiarity of this story's names, it quickly becomes apparent that *A Christmas Carol* is a story of how the dead can return to influence the living. Such influence was known in the nineteenth century by a single word: *spiritualism*.

Spiritualism began as a formal movement in, of all places, western New York. What is now seen as a farming region dotted with small towns was referred to, in the nineteenth century, as the "burned-over district" of America. The name refers to the power of the Second Great Awakening in that area that set people on fire with religious passions in the early nineteenth century. So strong was the fervor of religious fire that it was said to have intellectually burned over the entire region. In its extreme, the relationship of an individual to God is so strong that the role of organized churches becomes secondary, if not superficial. This is when new ideas representing all aspects of the moral, religious and spiritual spectrum found root in towns like Batavia, Rochester and Chautauqua.

In 1826, William Morgan, a printer and resident of Batavia, New York, was killed reportedly by a band of Freemasons. They were seeking retribution on Morgan, who had threatened to publish their secret ceremonies. What was arguably a local police matter escalated into a national political and social movement with a goal of banning all secret societies. So visceral was the belief that such groups needed to be eliminated that the Anti-Masonic Party—America's first third party—was established. Members of the party objected to Freemasonry on the grounds that its members used the secret society to conduct illicit business. Morally, many also objected to both the taking of oaths and the universal spirituality of the movement.

At the same time in a different part of New York, America's largest and most successful homegrown faith was established. Joseph Smith established in 1830 the Church of Jesus Christ of Latter-day Saints. Like others of his generation, Smith was caught up in the religious fervor of the Second Great Awakening. He also was fascinated by the ceremonies and history of the Freemasons, so he joined a local Masonic lodge. Not long after, Smith announced to the world that he had been directed by an angel to find and then translate tablets written by the ancient historian Mormon. The account linked the lost tribes of Israel to American Natives, thus providing a link from the ancient world to the New World. Smith's followers expanded, and he eventually left New York for Illinois, where he was killed by an angry mob. Eventually, his literal and spiritual descendants—the LDS Mormons—settled in Utah.

All of this religious fervor in western New York culminated, at least for our story, with the three Fox sisters: Leah, Maggie and Kate. In 1848, the two youngest sisters, Maggie and Kate, were living with their Methodist parents in Arcadia Township in western New York. The two reportedly began experimenting with a unique form of communication with the dead. The process, known as spirit rapping, involved specific mysterious knocks that were given in reply to questions asked by the sisters. The Fox home was said to be haunted by someone who had been murdered on the property, and their spirit was said to be the source of the knocking. As news of the spirit communication spread beyond the immediate Fox family, the girls' parents decided they should be sent to live with their eldest sister, Leah, in Rochester. Rather than quell the spirit rapping, all three daughters soon claimed to be able to communicate with spirits.

The stories of the Fox sisters spread in the region and found particular interest among the Quaker community. This was seemingly incongruous, as the strict and stern Quakers seemed to be the last group in which spiritualism could take root. Yet the Quakers, in this period, held many progressive ideas and considered the Fox sisters had received a divine gift in being able to communicate with the dead. Many Quakers were strongly influenced by the Second Great Awakening, so from a theological perspective, it was not a great leap to say that spiritualism was proof of God's help to humankind.

Leading thinkers of the time came to hear the Fox sisters speak and demonstrate their spirit rapping. Poet William Cullen Bryant and abolitionist Sojourner Truth were among the throngs who attended the sisters' programs in New York City. One frequent attendee was Horace Greeley. Arguably, the most celebrated newspaper publisher of the era, Greeley is best remembered for coining the phrase "Go west, young man, and grow up with the country." His fascination with the Fox sisters and the larger spiritualist movement drove him to provide extensive media coverage for the budding spiritualist movement. In 1888, Maggie confessed that the rapping was hoax that had been accomplished by her sisters cracking their knuckles to create the raps of the spirits. Even in the face of this revelation, however, many people continued to believe that the Fox sisters had been communing with spirits.

Others jumped onto the spiritualist bandwagon, and soon, a cottage industry sprang up around the real or purported abilities of people to speak with the dead. At the center of the spiritualist experience was a "medium," or the physical conduit between the world of the living and that of the dead. Each medium had specific spirit guide, often a Native, who would both provide direct counsel and seek information from other spirits. The methods of communication varied among mediums but could include table knocking or rapping, trumpet playing and, sometimes, the actual manifestations of

Mailed in 1952 from Lily Dale, the mysterious message suggests the sender was successful in communicating with a loved one from the other side.

spirits. The answers to the mediums' questions were often vague, reflecting the spirit's inability to focus clearly on the earthly plane. It should be said that a cynic—and there were many—might say the responses were vague to allow for interpretation to fit the response.

Spiritualism became so popular that there were how-to books published on how people could conduct their own séances if they were a budding medium. For those who wanted to lightly dip their spiritual toe in the water, there were Ouija boards, which were intended for home use. For the truly hardcore, there were those who sought answers from as many mediums as possible. A friend of mine is an example of the latter, as she tries new mediums every few weeks to get the answers she seeks. She is utterly devoted to the cause and is an absolute believer in the power of the spirit world. She and many others like her have found a common home for their beliefs in the Spiritualist Church.

The National Spiritualist Association of Churches (U.S.) and the Spiritualists' National Union (UK) are both associations made up of small constituent congregations who share a common set of beliefs about the role of spirits in the world. They use a Protestant-based religious service built around the belief of the "continuity of life and the existence of a spiritual universe." Spiritualist theology demands neither a belief in predestination nor a view that good works can secure a place in the afterlife. Their central tenet is that the afterlife is a continuum of the earthly spirit of the material world into the pure spirit of the spiritual world.

So, as it had been for anti-Masonry, Mormonism and a host of other movements, western New York became a home for the spiritualists. Just a few miles from Chautauqua is Lily Dale, the largest spiritualist cottage community in the United States. Founded in 1879, it remains a vibrant center for the practice and study of spiritualism.

Essentially, Lily Dale appears to be a small version of neighboring Chautauqua. The town is well planned, with wide streets bordered by summer cottages, and the properties are bisected by tree-lined common parks. A massive auditorium/tabernacle, along with a hotel, library, stores and food service, round out the community today.

One of the first elements that suggests this place is something different are the Leolyn Woods. Not only do the woods provide a protective greenway around the community, but the community prides itself on the fact that the trees are the last stand of original old-growth forest remaining in the state of New York. So massive and impressive are the woods that visitors often bring small homemade wooden houses to place in the woods for use by the tree fairies.

Close to the center of town is a truly impressive animal cemetery with elaborate homemade tombstones marking the final resting place of numerous generations of family pets. The role of animals in spiritualism is significant, as they are thought to have second sight and thus can perceive spirits that humans cannot see.

Just beyond the cemetery is a trail that leads to a large tree stump located in a small grove in the woods. If you come to this spot at specific times, one of the community's mediums will provide a reading and offer responses from the other side for people in attendance. They will publicly announce directed messages to people in the crowd from loved ones who have passed. Again, a modern cynic could easily argue that the messages are reflections of the intuitive sensitivity of the medium in figuring out the needs of the people in the crowd. Yet a believer would argue that the responses are based on totally unique knowledge that is available only to the spirit and their respective family member. The community acknowledges both interpretations in a way that neither the disbeliever nor the faithful are challenged. That live-and-let-live attitude about spiritualism makes Lily Dale a place where both the real and magical worlds collide.

To Remind You of Our
Many Pleasant Hours in

Lily Dale

Come Again

Left: This bold postcard was produced to advertise the Leolyn Hotel, located on the grounds of Lily Dale.

Below: The faithful are gathered in the auditorium at Lily Dale, probably to hear a program on table rapping, spirit trumpets or some other topic.

INTERIOR OF AUDITORIUM   LILY DALE, N. Y.

Following the same plan as other cottage communities, the houses in Lily Dale were arranged around common park land.

Walking Lily Dale's streets, one immediately notices that most cottages have a neatly hand-lettered sign in front that reads "Medium." The purpose of these signs is to inform the ticket-paying visitor that the cottage resident is available for a private spiritual reading. Cottage ownership in Lily Dale has the unique requirement that a potential resident must be a practicing and tested medium who is a member of the Spiritualist Church.

Each year, the Lily Dale Assembly provides a summer season of public programming. The programs are wide-ranging and reflect the hottest topics in spiritualism and the occult. In 2023, these programs covered topics from Asian mysticism and Feng Shui to the latest television ghost hunters speaking about their exploits. In the past, the programs focused more on séances and different forms of spirit communication. Interestingly, the Fox sisters' original cottage had been relocated to Lily Dale but sadly burned down some years before the writing of this book.

Fundamentally, all visitors have to ask themselves the question of whether they believe or not. Personally, I am a doubting Thomas on such topics, and yet I cannot explain why the doors on my car once suddenly began to violently lock and unlock while I was driving through the community. It has never happened before or since, and I have no explanation. So, perhaps it's all real?

The more widespread manifestation of spiritualist retreats were small camps like Silver Belle in Lancaster, Pennsylvania, and Freeville in New

York. Unlike Lily Dale, which operated with a large number of mediums, these camps were built on the charisma, spiritual talents and business acumen of a single medium/founder. When they were a strong leader, the spiritualist camp flourished. However, if the founder died, there was a scandal or the camp got too big to be well managed, the community usually fragmented and closed.

For an ambitious medium, developing a camp was one of the best ways to attract followers. It did require considerable financial backing and an acumen for hospitality services. A talented medium could use their ability to leverage financial backers who would give or loan them money to start the community. The first task was then to secure a camp location. Hotels were the ideal locations, as they could accommodate lectures, spiritualist church services and séances. In particular, large Victorian hotels were the most popular, as they had both the right "look" and were relatively inexpensive to purchase. While the plumbing was primitive, the bedrooms small and there was a near constant risk of fire, such hotels were cheap and readily available to house spiritualist communities.

One such place was the former Ephrata Mountain Springs Hotel, constructed in 1848 around a natural mineral spring and located in northern Lancaster County, Pennsylvania. It had been the brainchild

The Forest Temple is one of several locations where guests can receive messages relayed by mediums.

of Joseph Konigmacher, a sometime Pennsylvania state senator and prominent local businessman. While the hotel business did not survive long past the death of Konigmacher, the building remained perched on a hill, overlooking the town of Ephrata. The building was big and rambling, perfect for the right new owner. John and Mary Stephan were Ephrata residents and interested spiritualists. In the winter, the Stephans went to a spiritualist camp in Florida, where they became friends with the owners: Ethel Post and her husband, Myron.

Ethel Post was a highly regarded spiritualist and medium who had a large following in Florida. While the details are unclear, it appears that the Stephans and Posts joined forces to create a new spiritualist camp based in Ephrata. The decision to move was based on several reasons. First, Florida in the summer was stinking hot, so the mountains of Pennsylvania were ideal for a cool retreat. Second, the town of Ephrata and the Konigmachers' old hotel had been a destination for visitors harkening back to the mineral spring era, so there was existing tourism infrastructure. Third, Ephrata was within fifteen miles of three successful cottage communities: the Pennsylvania Chautauqua, the Mount Gretna Campmeeting and the Mount Lebanon Camp Meeting. While the spiritualist community was never connected to these other communities, their proximity meant that

Camp Silver Belle, Ephrata, Pa.

25976-C

Although it is difficult to see in this postcard from 1944, Camp Silver Belle lurks behind the trees and porches.

there were local vendors who could help to supply the new spiritualist camp. Finally, like icing on a cake, the town's most celebrated attraction was a former early eighteenth-century mystical community known as the Ephrata Cloister. Founded by Johann Conrad Beissel, the Ephrata Society attracted both celibates and families who came to live, work and worship along the banks of Cocalico Creek. Beissel was incredibly charismatic and preached a unique theology that attracted many in its day. Ephrata was a mystical and beautiful place that was perfect for a new spiritualist camp.

The Stephans and Posts held the first spiritualist camp meeting in 1932 at a small public park in town. Overnight guests stayed at the local Ephrata Hotel. The community was not happy. Outsiders coming in and preaching spiritualism rubbed locals the wrong way. To make matters worse, there was a scandal about how the arrangement for the use of the park had been made. It appeared to many that the Stephans and Posts had used backdoor tactics to take the park for their use. The situation festered until the Posts acquired the old and long-empty Mountain Springs Hotel and moved their camp into its long, dusty halls. Called Camp Silver Belle, it would become a local landmark.

From its founding, the spiritualist movement had strong ties to both the feminist and suffragist movements. This was due in part to their proximity, since the first gathering of women to advocate for women's issues occurred in 1848 in western New York, not far from where the Fox sisters lived. The freethinkers who embraced feminism were often the same who sought out knowledge at a Chautauqua or who might attend a séance. It was a time when women were being empowered by both new educational opportunities and access to political leaders. Sojourner Truth, the formerly enslaved woman turned abolitionist leader, is one such an example of this. Escaping from slavery in New York, she was the first woman to successfully sue to be reunited with her son, who was held in slavery. She went on to become a leader in the feminist movement, and she also attended several séances.

The spiritualist movement attracted many women to its ranks as mediums. While many have argued that they were spiritually in-tune and thus made excellent mediums, many women found economic and personal independence in operating professionally as a medium. It was a far more interesting career for many women than teaching school or serving as a nurse. A great example of such a woman was the founder of Camp Silver Belle: Ethel Post Parrish. She was an incredibly successful businesswoman, a noted medium who had a national reputation and someone who also had a complex private life that bordered on the scandalous. And despite having her reputation damaged over the years by sensationalist discoveries about her work as a medium, her biographer notes that her business acumen alone made her among the most remarkable women of her time.

Like all good biographies, hers contains some mystery around her early years. Her birth year is unknown, and she grew up in a Quaker family who were early followers of spiritualism. Divorced twice at an early age, she then married her third husband, Myron Post, who helped build and expand her following. After building Silver Belle, she divorced Post and remarried a much younger man within a week of the judge issuing her divorce decree.

Ethel first came to the attention of the public as a medium who was accurate in her readings. However, she soon expanded from answering questions to encountering more physical aspects of spirit manifestations. First was the use of a device called a spirit trumpet, which sounded magically in response to posed questions. When that seemed too tame, Ethel was able to conjure up ghostly voices that mysteriously responded to specific questions. Finally, at the peak of her career, while in a trance, she was able to manifest her spirit guide, Princess Silver Belle, who physically appeared and spoke to those assembled. For her believers, this was both the ultimate test and conclusive proof of her skills as a medium.

For those skeptics, the darkened room filled with individuals desperate to believe in spirit communication seemed fertile ground for trickery. The more elaborate Ethel's manifestations, the louder the cry came from skeptics for real proof of the sounds and figures actually emanating from the spirit world. In response, professional photographer Jack Edwards was invited to attempt to capture on film the manifestations during one of Ethel's séances. At the appointed hour, Parrish appeared and went into a trance while seated in her "cabinet." The latter was a small, elevated and curtained area located in front of the séance participants. Once she was in a trance, the manifestation of her spirit guide occurred. At that moment, Edwards took a series of time-lapse photographs of Parrish in her trance and the area surrounding her spirit cabinet.

Upon development, the images showed a ghostly figure shrouded in mist next to the cabinet. For the believers, this was the ultimate proof. The mist was ectoplasm that emanated from Ethel and connected her to Prince Silver Belle.

To a modern eye, it is clear that the negatives were manipulated with the addition of both a cutout figure of the "princess" and strands of cotton to create the ectoplasm. In effect, it was a primitive version of photoshopping an image. The power of belief is strong, so while each camp believed the other was wrong, the debates about the celebrated Silver Belle photographs raged for decades. The real benefit was, to paraphrase the old marketer's line, there was no such thing as bad publicity. Ethel's standing in the spiritual community rose dramatically after the photographs were published. She had been baptized by the fire of publicity, and to her faithful followers, she had proven herself and validated their beliefs.

Several years later, a second set of photographs, this time taken apparently without Parrish's knowledge, revealed something more nefarious. A woman confederate was shown hiding behind the cabinet's curtains and manipulating the spiritual trumpet, as well as producing other various spiritual activities. When published, these photographs proved much harder to explain. On top of these new photographs, Parrish found herself caught in a financial scandal. There had been a significant difference between the fees that she was paying to her speakers at Camp Silver Belle and the money collected from those who attended the programs. She stood accused of price gouging.

In any other community, such embarrassments might have destroyed her work and closed the camps. However, Ethel remained focused on the operations of her facilities in Florida and Pennsylvania and serving as a medium. Her personal charisma and talents were so great that the doubters among the spiritualist community and the public forgave her. Her camps flourished.

Ethel died in 1958, and it was assumed that Silver Belle would close shortly thereafter. However, the camp remained in operation first under her son and then under other owners until 1989. The longevity of the operation was clearly a tribute to the tenacity and business acumen of Ethel. The end of the camp came only because of the overall waning of the spiritualist movement in the 1980s and the rising costs of maintaining the old hotel year-round.

I interviewed several long-time residents about their experiences and knowledge of Camp Siler Belle. Most knew about the early hostility toward the camp over the land issues. Those who had strong religious convictions objected to the entire camp on theological grounds. However, to many in the outside world, Silver Belle was regarded as a local curiosity. Gerry Lestz, a noted Lancaster newspaper columnist and historian, related much of the more recent history of the camp to me before his passing. He noted that most locals enjoyed going there for Saturday or Sunday lunches, as the food was quite good. He also remembered Ethel would suddenly appear to walk among the tables and talk to the guests. He said she was friendly but "a bit odd."

Nationally Renowned   1932–1973

Silver Belle

Ephrata, Penna.   Phone 733-2503

Historically Famous

**MOUNTAIN
SPRINGS
HOTEL,
INC.**

1753 🔔 1973

Silver Belle Association Presents
an Outstanding Array of Internationally Known
Lecturers - Teachers - World Famous Psychics

Left: The program for the 1973 season at Camp Silver Belle lists a full program schedule, including readings, healing services and lectures.

Below: The spiritualist camp in Freeville, New York, was a small community with only modest buildings (shown in this photograph). The overgrown look suggests that the camp may have been short-lived.

FREEVILLE, N. Y.
Auditorium, Spiritualist Camp Grounds

With the closing of the camp, the contents of the hotel were auctioned off in a series of public sales. The building itself returned to being the same white elephant it had been since the Konigmacher heirs closed it in the early twentieth century. Sitting dark and alone in a grove of trees on a hill overlooking the town, its appeance and history seemed to be something right out of a Gothic novel. Eventually, it was torn down, although many in the community still speak about it in the present tense—as though both the spirits of its guests and the building are still present.

The spiritualist camps were a unique subset of the much larger cottage community movement. Their audiences were unique, devoted and arguably a bit shy about their involvement in the spiritualist movement. Spiritualism as a movement has had its ebbs and flows of interest by the larger society over the decades. It is that intense desire that we all have to both know what happens after death and hope that we can find personal resolutions with those who have passed.

Most of the camps are now gone, although Lily Dale remains strong and vibrant. It is a place where one—even if they are the most hardened cynic—can openly ask those questions that haunt us all about what happens after death. Prior to his death, Houdini gave his wife a special code that, if a medium shared with her, would be proof of life after death. The message never came, and yet people still gather on the anniversary of the great magicians' death in the hopes they will hear it.

8

CREATING THE COTTAGE COMMUNITY

Jumping into that imaginary time machine and going back to a given moment in the past is something most of us dream about doing. It's great fun to pretend about what life was like in the past. Ask any re-enactor why they dress up as soldiers, sailors or camp followers. And of course, the corollary of witnessing history as a time traveler was the question: What point in the past could a modern person live in successfully? A host of authors from Mark Twain (*A Connecticut Yankee in King Arthur's Court*) to Gene Roddenberry ("City of the Edge of Forever," in *Star Trek*) have written stories to inspire our imaginations about time travel.

Geeky historians are not immune to such daydreaming. I recall in graduate school having a debate with fellow students about what was the specific moment in the past when a modern person was unable to live because life at that point was so different from what it is today. After much discussion, the consensus was that 1890, plus or minus a few years, was the point in which the modern world began, and therefore, a present-day time traveler could function then. Such exercises represent the overthinking folly of graduate students, but the lesson is important to us. The 1890s were the period when the modern world was born. Technology and culture had reached a point of convergence with the modern world in those years.

This was also one of the most change-filled periods in human existence. The power of the steam/gas/electric engine, literally and metaphorically, affected everything from global transportation to farming. Medical improvements extended lifespans and saved both battlefield and accident

Tabernacles and auditoriums were among the first buildings to be modernized in cottage communities. Electricity allowed events to continue into the evenings, and ceiling fans helped keep everyone cool on August nights.

victims. New inventions and innovations, such as indoor plumbing, electric lights and movies, all became everyday by the 1920s. Beginning in the 1890s, a substantial part of the population was living longer and better than the wealthiest had just fifty years earlier. It was, to paraphrase Paul Simon, the original "age of miracle and wonder."

The changes that led to this modern world did not come easily or without a price. Mechanization and pressures for the faster delivery of goods led to dangerous working conditions that, in turn, resulted in organized labor unions. Strikes followed as workers sought better pay, safer workplaces and shorter workweeks. Writers like Upton Sinclair and Ida Tarbell established the literary proposition that for every shop with unsafe and unsanitary working conditions, there was a corresponding threat to public health. Sinclair's 1906 book *The Jungle* was a vivid exposé of the horrific conditions found inside the midwestern meatpacking industry. Sinclair took the unique approach of showing how the effects of poor working conditions resulted in rotten meat and watered-down milk for everyone. This news was shocking to digest, both metaphorically and literally, and resulted in reforms in meatpacking that spilled over into other industries.

Technological changes in this period impacted the daily lives of every American household. Looking at a Sears and Roebuck Company catalogue from the turn of the century, one finds advertisements for a host of newly invented and highly touted "modern" household appliances. Vacuums, washing machines and new household chemicals were all promoted as labor-saving devices. Moreover, what would one do with that extra time? One could pursue nobler purposes in life, such as art, music or humanitarian causes. The irony of this marketing was that it did not drive women to nobler pursuits; instead, it raised the bar of domestic cleanliness. Needing to ensure that your clothing was "whiter than white and brighter than bright" became the chief goal. The phrase "a clean home is a welcoming home" was created.

The focus on cleanliness generated by authors and the media resulted in substantial changes to how people decorated their homes. In the nineteenth century, people used long wool strip carpets in their rooms. Their bold patterns and colors became a staple of Victorian parlors. With the new twentieth century's focus on cleanliness, wall-to-wall carpeting was removed, as it was unsanitary. Instead, the new choice for a home was the use of area rugs on bare wooden floors. Such rugs were intended to be moved and cleaned separately, leaving the floor to then be vacuumed or mopped. This new standard of cleanliness was how a wholesome home needed to be maintained. Similarly, white paint became a norm for interior and exterior household use. It was the obvious symbolic choice of purity. Further maintaining it was a sign of wealth, insofar as it got dirty faster than any other color of paint.

Summer cottages, many of which were built in this period, became centerpieces for this new look. The roots of the clean modern cottage began with the overall planning of the cottage community. Running household water, a public sewer service and buried electric lines became the norm. These innovations were not just about public good; they were also good for marketing the cottage communities. One such example can be found in the Victorian novel titled *Ida Norton or Life at Chautauqua*, by Reverend T.L. Flood. This confection of historical fiction tells the story of a young girl and her experiences attending a Chautauqua. While it is a bit challenging to read today, the book is a clear homage to Chautauquas and the mental, physical and spiritual health they promoted.

Sing Sing, Round Lake and Ocean Grove camp-grounds possesses the refinement and the comforts of pleasant home society. And their life in the grove is so agreeable and healthy that thousands hasten from the cities to spend the summer months in rural retreats. Thus the camp ground has come to be in some respects of the summer home of many families. As a consequence, the elements of recreation and social life have become a permanent characteristic of the camp.[14]

Flood was by no means the only author to identify cleanliness and good health with cottage communities. J. Horace McFarland made the case for Eagles Mere as a healthy destination by informing readers of his promotional history of the community that he had personally paid to have the water in the lake tested for purity. The results, not surprisingly, were that the lake was pure and clean.

While testing lake water and having lots of trees spoke volumes to guests about the cleanliness of the community, there was the need to invest in infrastructure to keep it that way. In 1905, Ocean Grove, New Jersey, spent substantial amounts of its annual budget on installing a public water system. The benefits were obvious, as it provided for the health of residents and guests. However, not all of these public improvements were visible. In fact, one was only conscious of a good water system when they heard of someone in a nearby community who had gotten sick because of bad water. Therefore, the question came up about how the community could demonstrate the value of expensive infrastructure to the community. The answer was: use the clean water to create a green and dust-free community. Tree and grass watering was encouraged on both public and private grounds. To complete the look, a truck was hired and then dispatched through the town on a daily basis to hose down the dusty streets.

Clean water was just the tip of the infrastructure iceberg. The muckrakers had explained to Americans in their books and articles that drinking water downstream from where the cattle went to the bathroom was a bad idea. For the new cottage communities, this meant investing in a sanitation system on a large scale. In 1909, Ocean Grove and nearby Asbury Park jointly completed a sewer system that ran the towns' waste out through a standpipe into the ocean. While this would now be regarded as poor environmental planning, it was a substantial improvement over household cesspits.

These civic improvements for cottage owners did not necessarily address the problem of huge numbers of day visitors. Dust-free streets and green trees were wonderful, but what about sewage back-ups? That was the conundrum created by having so many day visitors. In addition, while the day visitors paid an admission fee for the privilege of being in the community, the revenue did not keep up with the costs of maintaining the needed summer infrastructure. For communities like Ocean Grove, whose beaches and boardwalks attracted thousands of day visitors, a serious issue caused tensions. The problem was exacerbated by the local businesses that thrived on the meals and souvenirs sold to the day visitors. More guests, not fewer, was what they sought. There was no clear solution to the problem. Addressing managed access for some cottage communities took on a more odious note. In Ocean Grove's annual report, it was noted:

> *Multitudes crowd our precincts: they from various localities, in some of which there prevails contagious disease. Many of these persons bring in their systems the germs of diseases. While here they disregarded proper hygiene, and violate the laws of health, and the result, their own sickness, and the endangering of the heath of the community and thus spread disease in the town.*[15]

Another area of public friction was the topic of public transportation. Pitman had a long history of tensions between the year-round residents, summer cottage residents, day visitors to the camp meeting and those who came to nearby Alycon Park. Each of these groups clamored for space on local train service, and each resented the other for taking up space. Similarly, Mount Gretna had to deal with Chautauqua residents, camp meeting residents and day visitors to each community, summer park visitors and then the annual encampment of the Pennsylvania National Guard. Trains ran frequently, but this did not stop the complaints. The camp meetings, in particular, were vehement about prohibiting Sunday train service.

Once at their cottages, families had to adjust to the complexity of squeezing into a small house with ongoing scrutiny from the neighbors who were only a few feet away. Cooking, in particular, was not easy because of spatial challenges. For a large family, there was the question of not only where to store the food but also where to cook and then eat it. Many of the advertisements for cottage building plans promoted built-in furnishings that could, with a few machinations, be converted to suit another use. For example, you could convert a bunk bed into a table or a bench. It undoubtedly seemed like a fun novelty at first, but I suspect it soon became a challenge to manage both meals and bedtime and the corresponding need to shift furniture.

An even more pressing issue was access to fresh food, since both household and community food storage was limited. Remembering that cottage communities were used in the summer, when heat rapidly spoiled food, this was a serious problem. The governing associations were well aware of these challenges and developed an extensive roster of vendors who often paid

Common public wells were features in older cottage communities. They were gathering places where residents could catch up on the latest news.

the association rent to set up and sell both raw and prepared food. South Seaville Camp Meeting had a long list of food providers, including one who ran an oyster stand throughout the summer season.

Another critical element of cottage design was ventilation. Most cottages were constructed with large double-hung windows that opened on all sides of the building. Those on the front of the house often went from floor to ceiling to provide optimal ventilation. Thankfully, the advent of window screens after 1868 dramatically reduced the passage of flies, bats and birds indoors. Air movement was critical, but on a hot and still night after a sunny and hot day, sleeping became a challenge. To solve that problem, most cottages had sleeping porches. These were located on the second floor and were heavily screened so the family could escape the bugs, heat and neighbors. On hot nights, the entire family might sleep outside. Summer cottages that did not have second floors would occasionally have sleeping porches built on the side, although privacy was a concern.

Daily life in a summer cottage community revolved around four big blocks of time. The longest, quite naturally, was reserved for sleeping and eating and included meal preparation. Next was the time spent attending the various formal summer programs. Camp meetings and Chautauquas

Seasonal buildings had ventilation challenges. Here, a tabernacle at a camp meeting has incorporated hinged window coverings to allow the building to be fully opened to enhance the airflow.

The cottage of Mrs. Thomas A. Edison at Chautauqua is the perfect example of all the different ways a homeowner could keep cool. The porches on the first and second floors, as well as at the rear, provided space for both entertaining and sleeping.

Some of the many activities offered in Chautauquas were cooking classes.

generally ran their summer programs for at least three weeks a season, but some varied. Classes were scheduled in the mornings, while larger programs and concerts were held in the afternoons and evenings. Weekends, particularly in camp meetings, were times for religious services. It goes without saying that the length of time for the service was directly proportionate to the level of religious intensity within the community.

The third segment of time in a cottage community was devoted to recreation. Postcard images show that going for walks in the woods or on the beach was the preferred recreational option in every community. For communities like Pitman or Mount Gretna that abutted public or private parks, the options were extensive. At Mount Gretna, the park area surrounding the communities had elaborate paths and bridges for walking.

Swimming in a lake or ocean was, of course, a high point of cottage life, particularly among the children. Most cottage communities owned a water feature or provided access like South Seaville to the ocean. There were also formal structured recreational opportunities at many of the communities. Mount Gretna had tennis courts that remain a staple of the community's summer season. Postcards again provide us clues about other recreational activities, as they illustrate scenes of lawn bowling, volleyball and, of course, strolling and talking.

View Camp Meeting Grounds, Newton Hamilton, Pa.

Relaxation was part of cottage community life, as exemplified by the hammocks and benches for the residents of the Newton Hamilton Camp Meeting.

The final block of dedicated time was used by family members to attend one or more of the various social clubs that met during the season. Someone once said that America is a nation of joiners, and certainly, the abundance of summer cottage clubs confirms that notion. Regardless of the type of cottage community, most were church and/or missionary based. The most popular were the Sunday schools that included children's Bible study programs and adult teacher training. These were at the heart of the Chautauqua and camp meeting movements. Not that distant in popularity were missionary support clubs. These entities raised money to support overseas missionary work and provided a venue for former missionaries to come and speak. Finally (but of immense importance), there was the Woman's Christian Temperance Union (WCTU).

Today, the temperance movement seems like a bit of a joke, as adult beverages are so common in the mainstream that few people think about a time when they were totally outlawed. Yet temperance, with the WCTU at its chief cheerleader and proponent, was one of the largest and most widespread movements of the twenteith century. Founded in 1874, the WCTU found fertile ground among the membership of the Methodist and Presbyterian churches. By the 1890s, the organization had announced—and no one was arguing—that it was the largest women's organization in the world. In my family, a maiden great-aunt was a local and state leader of the WCTU. When she died in the 1930s, more than one hundred women, all dressed in black and carrying wreaths, arrived by train to attend the services held in the front parlor of her home. For our family, the irony of this story was that her brother made applejack whiskey for the community in their shared basement.

The WCTU's influence peaked in 1919 with the adoption of the Eighteenth Amendment to the U.S. Constitution, which prohibited the sale of intoxicating liquors. Their victory empowered these strong women to address other social issues. Their influence was that much greater since none of the women members had the right to vote. Many in the WCTU saw the injustice of this issue and pivoted their political attention toward women's suffrage. A smaller number went further and became active in the cause of universal feminism. The power of women as voters, albeit disenfranchised ones, resulted in the passage of the Nineteenth Amendment, which gave women the right to vote. The summer WCTU meetings in cottage communities were vital to these movements, as attendees shared ideas and strategies from communities all over a region. Speakers on temperance and suffrage were reassured their messages would resonate not just in the camp meeting but when the participants returned home.

There were many other clubs and social organizations in the cottage communities. In terms of the sheer number of clubs, the Chautauquas probably had the most per capita. Postcards from the period show men's clubs, garden clubs, sporting clubs and, in particular, art and music clubs. So popular were the latter that Chautauqua, New York, constructed permanent studies and rehearsal halls for use by artists and musicians.

A particularly unique entity was the Chautauqua Literary and Scientific Circle, shortened then and now to CLSC. Established by Chautauqua founder John Heyl Vincent, the CSLC was a four-year curriculum of classes envisioned to provide both a scientific and humanistic education. Complete with classes, exams and diplomas, the program could be accomplished either at home or at a Chautauqua. Its advertisements noted that it was a rigorous program intended to offer a convenient education for those whose time or financial resources would not allow them to go to a college. The program was incredibly popular and, in its time, bridged the gap between what we would consider secular and religious learning. As an example, the writings of Charles Darwin were taught as part of the CSLC curriculum. CSLC was a significant intellectual movement in America, as it was readily open to both men and

Shown on the left side of this postcard is the original CSLC building in Chautauqua, New York.

Finding the balance between education, spiritual growth, physical fitness and artistic endeavors was at the heart and soul of all the cottage communities. The Arts and Crafts building at Chautauqua in New York was typical of the permanent structures the communities built to promote elements of this diverse community life.

women. While universal education was common at the elementary and secondary levels, higher academic learning remained available to mostly men. The CLSC opened the doors for many women to gain access to the ideas presented as part of a college-level education.

Organizations like the CSLC and the WCTU provided unique opportunities for women in a time when defined gender roles were changing. Under the guise of educational opportunities, these communities served to foster a spirit of activism in women. For example, fighting and then winning the battle against alcohol resulted in a subsequent push for equality at the ballot box.

Education became the key for many women to move into the working world and away from traditional domestic life. The universal education promoted by the CSLC program in the 1920s led families to send their daughters to college. Now, thanks to the promotion of learning within the cottage communities, the notion is widely accepted.

9

COTTAGE STYLE

The Original Look

The summer cottage style has long been the subject of coffee table books and shelter magazine articles. Today, it is called "shabby chic," "cottagecore" or "stylishly worn." In the 1900s, cottage living was described as "picnic housekeeping." Coined by Ida Tarbell, a journalist and author, this term referenced the mixing of old and new furnishings to reflect the casual lifestyle of cottages. It was the notion of living every day as though you were at a picnic with odd furniture pulled up around a sawbuck table covered with an old, checked tablecloth, a pitcher of summer flowers sitting on it.

Tarbell's autobiography is one of the best sources of information on daily cottage life. She attended several sessions at Chautauqua as a girl in the 1890s and then returned later as an adult correspondent for the magazine the *Chautauquan*. As a result, her perspective as a writer is unique, as she had seen cottage life through the eyes of both a child and an adult. Her book *All in the Day's Work* describes cottage life in this way:

> You had them at it, out in the rear of their cottages, over an old wood stove or stone fireplace, the men in their shift sleeves, the women in big aprons, if not wrappers. Planks on sawhorses for tables, mats (we had not yet learned to say doilies), benches for seats. The natural practice of bringing discarded furniture from home to furnish the cottages led to the only distinctive piece of Chautauqua furniture I recall—a long high backed bench made from an old fashioned four-poster bedstead. There

This is arguably the quintessential example of a summer cottage. From the canoe hanging from the second-floor porch to the hammocks on the first, it speaks volumes about summer recreation.

were few garrets in all the country about Chautauqua that did not harbor one or more such bedsteads. They had been hidden away when families could afford the new oak or walnut bedroom suites. Some ingenious person discovered that shortening the sidepieces of a four-poster to seat width, using the headboard for a back, you had a commodious, and with cushions, a comfortable seat, even couch…[16]

The bed/bench that Tarbell describes was and is a common feature in many cottage communities, as well as older family farms. They were made by repurposing early nineteenth-century beds into seating furniture. The beds originally used a woven rope framework to support the mattress. When tied tight, such rope beds were not uncomfortable. However, if the ropes loosened or broke, then a good night's sleep could take a serious downward turn. So unreliable were the ropes that furniture makers replaced them with wooden slats, metal straps and, ultimately, box springs. By the Civil War, most rope beds were banished to the attic. They were then reworked in the 1890s to be used as benches at the summer cottage.

Photographs of the interiors of cottages are quite rare, but those that do survive show that Tarbell was correct in her assessment of picnic living. Most houses were furnished in a true mish-mosh of styles from the antique

This stereocard image shows the interior of a cottage from the 1880s. The furnishings mix old and new styles ranging from the 1860s balloon back chairs to the 1880s patent furniture folding chairs scattered in the room. The floor is covered in strip carpeting, and the walls are covered in a classical wallpaper.

to the contemporary. Whatever was in Grandma's attic was available for use in the cottage. This mixing of styles and periods was part of the charm of cottage living. It had the familiarity of home but could also stand up to a little wear and tear.

A brief note needs to be made about the term "cottage furniture." Historically it referenced late-1800s softwood furniture that was gaudily painted to resemble ebonized or bleached hardwood furnishings. What it lacked in terms of wood quality, it more than made up for in its decoration. Sold in bedroom suites, each piece was covered in a cream or taupe paint with stencils and free-hand decoration applied on top to simulate flowers, birds and other elements. While called "cottage furniture," most sets were made for hotels or boardinghouses. Its size alone made it impractical for inclusion in small cottages.

The size of a cottage was the most significant factor in dictating how one decorated. Most cottages had small bedrooms with even narrower hallways and still even smaller staircases. As a result, bedrooms could be fitted out with a bed, a side table, a washstand and a bureau—but little else. However, even with those items, they needed to be very narrow or easily broken down in order to navigate the stairs. Minimal was the rule on second floors.

Flooring and coverings varied depending on the location of the community. Oak was often used in cottages, as it was durable and somewhat resistant to water and insect damage. As noted, the earliest cottages used Victorian strip carpeting, as it was favored for most interiors. However, the influence of the Arts and Crafts movement after 1900 resulted in area rugs on hardwood floors becoming the preferred choice. One particularly interesting choice was the use of Navajo weavings. These brilliantly colored weavings were introduced to the Northeast during the last decades of the nineteenth century. A theatrical program from Mount Gretna from the 1930s included an advertisement for a cottage owner who was offering Navajo rugs for cottages. As recently as the 1990s, there was at least one Mount Gretna Chautauqua cottage that still had its original Navajo rugs on the floor.

Cottages did range in size, depending on their owners' wealth and the type of communities they were located in. Camp meetings usually had smaller houses, while some Chautauquas had homes that included formal dining rooms and even the occasional ballroom. Interestingly, even in the largest cottages, bedrooms remained remarkably small by modern standards. Homeowners spent their money on the public and family rooms rather than bedrooms. The singular element that was common to both large and small cottages was the need for an expansive front porch. The porches could be built in different configurations and sizes, but regardless, it had to be there. Porches were where one went to look at those passing by and to be seen by those looking in.

In looking at both large and small cottage communities throughout the Mid-Atlantic, there is a remarkable homogeneity in both the appearance and floorplan of the cottages. This is not unexpected, since almost all cottage designs were taken from pattern books. Popularized by builders, pattern books consisted of line drawings that showed different styles of houses along with rudimentary floorplans and room sizes. Often, a master list of materials accompanied these drawing so owners could estimate costs. Written and illustrated by architects and professional designers, these books were distributed to builders who, in turn, shared them with clients.

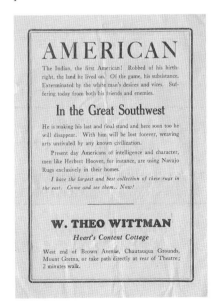

This advertisement for Native rugs on the inside of the Gretna Players' theater program from the 1920s illustrates the popularity of Navajo rugs in cottages.

Pattern books were the most popular way to construct a house. America was a young nation and, as a result, did not have an abundance of architects, the fastest and easiest resource for home building. For summer cottages, among the earliest and most popular pattern books was Andrew Jackson Downing's *The Architecture of Country Houses*, printed in 1853. Downing, who was both a solid architect and a great writer, produced a work that became the spiritual—if not literal—Bible for summer cottage construction for nearly a century. He established the philosophy behind summer cottage design:

> *The third reason is, because there is a moral influence in a country home—when, among an educated, truthful and refined people, it is an echo of their character—which is more powerful than any mere oral teachings of virtue and morality. That family, whose religion lies away from its threshold, will show but slender results from the best teachings, compared with another where the family hearth is a made a central point of the Beautiful and the Good.*[17]

From this premise, Downing began to focus on the need for quality materials to be used in construction, as well as the importance of style. To make his case, he evaluated historical styles of architecture through the ages before reaching the conclusion that the Gothic style was best suited for a country house. It "expresses as large a union of domestic feeling and artistic knowledge as any other known."[18] As vivid as his writing, Downing illustrated the book with drawings of Gothic cottages situated not in bare fields but rather surrounded by towering pine trees. It was a clear reference to the notion that among the trees was the morally correct place to raise a family.

Downing's writings caught on particularly in the Northeast, where abundant forests provided plenty of wood for cutting out the quatrefoils and pointed arches of Downing's Gothic building fantasies. So popular were his designs that they became the architectural embodiment of both camp meetings and Chautauquas, as they encapsulated the harmony between God and man. Of all his design elements, the steeply pitched roof of a Gothic cottage with a cut-out verge board and quatrefoil was the epitome of these cottages. His emphasis on decorative wood trim was intended to highlight the handcraftsmanship of the house. The irony was that the trim could be quickly mass-produced if thinner slabs of wood were obtained. No one could tell the difference from the ground, so vast numbers of sawmills

This is the quintessential example of Downing's vision for the Gothic house set into a woodland setting, albeit, in this case, it is right up against the neighboring Gothic house. The floor-to-ceiling windows on the first floor both matched Downing's vision and provided strong circulation of air.

began producing thin decorative trim. Downing soon became aware of the cheapening of his designs and warned against such work, as it would be "falling into the gingerbread character."[19]

The *Architecture of Country Houses* went through numerous editions and, interestingly, remains in print today. Its popularity can clearly be seen in the designs of the cottage communities in South Seaville and Mount Lebanon, where Gothic design is evident on most cottages. Even for those without distinctive Gothic elements, there is a certain homage to Downing's views. The planting of trees in proximity to each house, a feature found in every community, came directly from his writings. This passion for the treescape arguably is one of the most long-lasting successes of Downing's book.

By the late 1880s, other pattern books expanded on Downing's vision of Gothic cottage building. These later books were less severe in their designs than Downing was. Not everyone wanted to live in a miniature copy of Westminster Abbey. For example, architect S.B. Reed published in 1895 a pattern book titled *Cottage Houses for Village and Country Homes.* He makes no connections to any moral or spiritual ideology in the text but instead cuts right to the chase with architectural plans beginning on page 1. He illustrated everything from a three-room worker's cottage to a fourteen-room "French Roofed Cottage." The cottages' prices ranged from $2,500 for a French roofed cottage to under $200 for a simple one-story structure. The latter had two rooms, two closets and a porch. The advertisement, targeted at the camp meeting crowd, went on to note that this was far cheaper than renting a tent over the long term. Knowing the small scale of his cottages, Reed provided for numerous foldout storage, sleeping and dining options. Finally, he used a phrase that A.J. Downing would have loved: "A single low tree, with extended branches, may shade several cottages, and serve as support for swings and hammocks for the young folks."[20]

For the camp meetings, the Gothic style was eminently suitable. However, it was a tad severe, particularly for the cottage communities built more for recreation and less for religion. For the less religious communities, the Shingle Style became the cottage design of choice. Featuring an asymmetrical façade incorporating exuberant arches, angles and towers, Shingle Style buildings could be scaled for almost any lot size. The name shingle style came from the preferred use of alternating bands of differing wooden shingles used to side and roof the house. While its roots date from the end of the nineteenth century, the style remains preferred for "beach cottage architecture."

The intellectual origin of the shingle style began with Boston architect Henry Hobson Richardson. His designs called for the use of a wide range of building materials, including cut brownstone blocks that were fashioned into big, bold arches. Rooflines were complex and often utilized angular dormers. Named Richardsonian Romanesque, it was a style that was popular among the wealthy, as the stonework was very expensive and required highly skilled craftsmen. When worked in wood, however, Richardson's designs were altered and modified into the popular shingle style. The availability of wood and planing mills in the Northeast made the style ideal in cottage communities throughout the region. Eagles Mere and Mount Gretna feature some of the best inland examples of the style, while Ocean Grove has the beach version.

The last of the cottage architectural styles was the Adirondack cottage. Named for the Adirondack Mountains in northern New York, this style was a variant of the immensely popular bungalow that was the quintessential

The Shingle Style of building is arguably the unofficial style for most summer cottage communities. This house illustrates many of the style's design elements, including an asymmetrical façade, sprawling porches and a mixture of different-shaped shingles on the top floor. Lacking trees and shrubs, this cottage was probably just completed when the photograph was taken.

home of the Arts and Crafts movement. This all sounds like a lot of very complex arts and architectural mumbo jumbo, but it is, in fact, very simple.

The Arts and Crafts movement was born out of a desire to showcase handcraftsmanship in a time when society as a whole was becoming more and more dependent on the machine. The celebration of technology and industrial design in Victorian America rubbed many thinkers, artists and architects the wrong way. They saw the cheap machine-made goods as lacking in artistic soul. Instead, they encouraged the production of handmade items that physically showed the maker's tool marks. Copper kettles would be hand-hammered, and furniture would be pinned together with wooden dowels rather than nails. All of this was couched in architectural styles built on historic or exotic models.

Those historic revivals embodied both design and construction elements spanning more than five hundred years of artistry. For those devotees of the Arts and Crafts movement who lived west of the Mississippi, it was the artistry of the southwestern "mission style" that was popular in building. Coming from the Pacific Northwest, the Arts and Crafts architectural firm of Greene and Greene used design elements from Japan and China in its buildings. To the east of the Mississippi, the bungalow became the personification of the Arts and Crafts movement.

Named for a housing style that originally came from Bengal, India, bungalows usually have one floor with an open floorplan and wide porches. They were common to nearly every cottage community built after 1900, and plans were widely available in books and magazines. In the Northeast, designers modified the bungalow to accommodate local construction materials. These were bungalows that were constructed of logs or framing with thick wooden shingles. Often with side porches that featured unpeeled tree trunks as supports and rails, these were called Adirondack bungalows or cottages. Named after Nathaniel Hawthorne's beloved Leatherstocking country of northern New York, they were popular in the cottage communities located in western New York and Pennsylvania.

Adirondack cottages generally featured sweeping rooflines, bold woodwork and an open floorplan with minimal hallways. Interior finishes tended to be dark fumed or oiled oak. The Adirondack cottages were often clad in wooden shakes that, at first glimpse, appear related to the older Victorian shingle style. However, the shingles are very thick slabs that were robustly applied to the entire exterior, giving the house a truly rustic

The only identifier is a penned caption of "Bluebird Cottage Living Room." Probably dating to the 1920s, this room has an area rug in the center with plenty of bare wood flooring exposed around the perimeter. The furnishings are inexpensive wicker and oak bookcases. In the corner is a Victrola ready to be played.

appearance. In Mount Gretna, such buildings covered in these thick dark shakes were nicknamed "pinecone houses."

The final style of building to discuss is the portable cottage. While they occasionally incorporated decorative elements from the Gothic style, portable cottages were generally far simpler in design than Downing's original plans. They were popular in camp meetings where individual plots had to be rented from the association rather than privately owned. Having a portable cottage ensured that if things did not work out, one could take their house with them. While they were very pragmatic, portable cottages were not popular and are rarely seen today.

As noted, the singular common element for all summer cottages was the porch. They were seen by residents and guests as the most visible room in the house and accordingly reflected the style and taste of the occupants. Porches established a way for families to be both private and yet part of the larger community. One could read the newspaper or just as easily lean over and talk to their neighbor sitting on their porch or someone walking past their house.

Historians and folklorists have written extensively about "front porch culture," in which families engage with their communities from the front of their homes. It is a tradition that seems to leap many cultural borders, although its present influence has been much eroded by the more private "back deck." For cottage communities, porches were places where the adults could sit and talk, the young could play games on a rainy day and neighbors could congregate. It was also a way for families to show their prosperity. A newly painted porch with freshly painted furniture and a vase of gladiolas was a sign that the owner had both the time and money to spend on their "public room." Conversely, a porch that was rotting (a near constant issue) and filled with broken furniture suggested the family was neither prosperous nor, by implication, clean or morally upright. There is also an interesting argument to be made that porch size, location and placement were all executed intentionally to showcase the status of an owner.

The old real estate adage that buying a house is all about location, location and location was certainly true in cottage communities. Those homes that faced the tabernacle or auditorium were certainly the most desirable. Why? At the heart of most cottage communities was the tabernacle or auditorium. It was where the community gathered for events ranging from public meetings to church services and large public lectures. As such, it is probably no coincidence that the cottages closest to the tabernacle frequently have two-story porches as well as the most elaborate decorative trim.

West Ave. in the Grove, Pitman, N. J.

The gardens in front of these cottages in Pitman illustrate the use of tolerant annuals, creeping vines and large trees that were the hallmarks of cottage communities.

Cottage communities had numerous other public buildings as well. The Chautauquas, as centers of learning, had "halls" dedicated to the arts or philosophy. These halls were also used for smaller lectures and programs. Invariably, these halls were constructed to appear as small versions of ancient Greek temples like the Parthenon in Athens. Unlike their ancient ancestors, however, the Chautauqua versions were usually fully enclosed to keep out the rain and bugs. The choice of such architecture was simple. The ancients were thought to have done their teaching in such structures, so it made sense that modern teachers should conduct their classes in a copy. Today, great examples of "modern" Greek temples can be found in Mount Gretna and Chautauqua, where they are still used. Such buildings, however, were an anathema to the church camp meetings, where planners and clergy alike noted that the ancients were pagans, and thus, such buildings were not suited for a Christian community.

Dormitories were another common public structure found in camp meetings. These buildings grew out of the tent meeting tradition and were used for small families, couples or singles who needed affordable accommodations. Architecturally, the dormitories were usually rambling and nondescript one- and two-story buildings. Today, few survive, as they generally do not meet fire code and are often too small for modern use. Brandywine Summit and South Seaville retain their dormitories.

A cafeteria or dining hall was another public building found in most of the cottage communities. They were generally long horizontal buildings with window screening on all sides. A kitchen was built into one end, and meals were served either family style or through a buffet line. Dining halls were where families could socialize in a more informal way and were thus frequently written about in histories of the cottage communities. In recent decades, many have been modified into enclosed picnic pavilions, often with a snack bar at one end selling hot dogs and ice cream. One of the best surviving examples of a dining hall is located in Mount Lebanon. Its survival is due in part to the long-standing community tradition of serving good meals.

In the horse-drawn wagon era, all the cottage communities were heavily reliant on fields and sheds for grazing and keeping animals. Maintaining the fields was not easy for the communities, as there needed to be both good water and ample grass, along with a system for managing the manure. At the same time, there was an equally large challenge for the storage of carriages and wagons. They needed to be shaded from the sun under the trees but not in a place where they could easily be hit by falling limbs during a summer storm. This was a challenge, and often, communities hired farriers for the season to deal with horse shoeing and the odd carriage repair.

When the automobile era arrived, many of the grazing and carriage fields were either converted into parking areas for cars or sold off to raise revenue. The challenge with the new iron horses was that they needed hard roads to drive and park on, which meant communities needed to relandscape. For summer owners/residents, garages were soon built to protect expensive cars. And the farrier was soon replaced by automotive mechanics. Today, South Seaville and Malaga retain a number of open fields close by that were probably used for grazing animals. The Mount Gretna Campmeeting has an intact street of garages that were built over the decades for residents.

A final element found in some cottage communities, particularly Chautauquas and spiritualist camps, were hotels. These were generally large and rambling buildings with several multistoried wings and a dining room. The top floor, attic or one wing was reserved for staff, since the work was seasonal. By modern standards, these hotels would be considered primitive, with their small rooms and communal bathrooms on each floor. Some of the beach hotels used just louvered or slatted doors on rooms to allow for ventilation. As building codes changed and there was an increased concern about fire, a majority of these hotels closed. Today, the Maplewood Hotel in Lily Dale, New York, remains one of the most intact cottage community hotels.

This 1911 postcard view of the Mount Gretna Inn shows a nearly textbook example of an Arts and Crafts room. The oldest item is the oil banqueting lamp in the corner, and the newest is probably the electric table lamp in the foreground. The floor has area rugs, and the walls were covered in either fabric or paper. The Chinese hanging lantern is typical of the Arts and Crafts taste and cottage living.

While it's dated to 1955, the room's décor is right out of the 1930s. The wicker furniture and area rugs harken back to the older Arts and Crafts style, while the overstuffed sofa is probably the newest item. Also note the vases with gladiolas in them.

Summer cottage living was fundamentally about coming together with family, friends and strangers to create a "new" community based on shared ideas. While many cottage communities drew attendees from the same communities where they lived year-round, it was not an exclusive subset. Cottage residents might also come from neighboring counties or states. Thus, an important part of cottage life was learning to make new friends among summertime neighbors. Thus, having a living room—the front porch—that looked out on the world was a great way to meet neighbors. Common wells and dining halls were also about making new friends. All were intended to develop a new community very quickly as families gathered for the summer season.

10

THE MODERN COTTAGE

The continuing popularity of the cottage look today is unmistakable. Books, shelter magazines and a host of YouTube videos are available to show you how to build, rehabilitate, restore, renovate, redesign and redecorate a beach house, mountain home or even an Upper East Side apartment in the cottage style. For the young, there is the current "cottagecore" style that incorporates rural cottage aesthetics into personal fashion and home décor. Suffice to say, the cottage look has never gone out of style. It remains as timeless as the cottage communities themselves.

So, what are the key decorating elements of a classic cottage? Assuming one has a cottage, it starts with the exterior paint. The truly traditional cottage exterior was always painted white, with the trim contrastingly painted in either a hunter or forest green. Trim consisted of the porch railings, shutters and any decorative elements, such as the facing boards located beneath the roofline. The white and green scheme can be traced to the nineteenth-century notion that these colors represented both cleanliness (white) and nature (green). Today, the most widespread use of this paint scheme can be found at South Seaville, Malaga and Mount Lebanon, where probably 80 percent of the cottages are painted in this white and green scheme.

At the opposite end of the exterior paint spectrum are the cottages whose owners have drawn their inspiration from the Victorian "painted lady" look. The style got its name from the classic book by Elizabeth Pomada and Michael Larsen titled *Painted Ladies: San Francisco's Resplendent Victorian*, published in 1978. When it first appeared, the book revolutionized Victorian home restoration color palettes. Pomada and Larsen's research pointed out that the black-and-white photography of the nineteenth century could not capture the truly vibrant color scheme of houses. Years of study after carefully removing and examining the paint history in the accumulated coats from several buildings revealed a breathtaking use of a complex array of colors. Preservationists soon began to repaint Victorian houses in these newly rediscovered brilliant color schemes. The public soon began to call these houses "painted ladies," and the name stuck. The acceptance of these paint schemes has now become the norm for many contemporary cottage owners. Today, canary yellow, cotton candy pink and horizon blue are among the favorites. This look is particularly popular among the seaside cottage communities in places like Ocean Grove and its inland cousin Pitman.

As important as the paint is for the cottage, the right landscaping is vital. It all starts with the tree canopy. Providing both natural cooling for cottages as well as a visible link between man, nature and God, trees were a critical part of every community. Most of the trees one sees today were planted either at the time of individual cottage construction or to replace those subsequently lost due to storms or disease. Contrary to contemporary folklore, it does not appear that individual cottages were "fitted in" among the existing trees on a site. This would have made the builder's task nearly impossible because of both the roots and the limbs. Rather, a site would have been completely cleared to allow for both the transport and laying out of construction materials, as well as for the construction. Period images of newly built cottages frequently show newly planted trees but rarely proximate large ones. White pine, black oak, tulip poplars and ash were the most common choices. Although chestnuts and elms were equally common, most have since been lost to disease. Interestingly, the passion for trees was so great that many of the newly planted saplings were located very close to these communities' houses. In fact, these trees are so close that many have grown up and into cottages. The cottage that I owned at Mount Gretna Campmeeting had such a tree that invaded the roofline of the house, and it was doing quite well.

Today, most community associations actively manage their tree-scapes to prevent dead or diseased trees from falling and hitting the cottages. They have a regular replacement schedule for stressed trees and often have a plan for introducing new disease-resistant species into the landscape. The trees are an odd dichotomy for many cottage residents and associations. They remain central to why they exist and, of course, serve purposes to cool houses in the summer. Yet they can destroy houses, power lines and cars with one good windstorm. The money spent on the trees' ongoing care confirms that the former outweighs the latter in the minds of most.

This dense tree canopy also impacts the choice of foundation plantings because of both the shade and also the acidic loam from shed leaves or pine needles. New cottage owners learn about this very quickly, as most race out to purchase and plant geraniums, zinnias and sunflowers soon after moving in during the spring. As the trees leaf out, the sun-loving annuals wither and die. As with any new house, the first step in landscape planning is to do absolutely nothing outdoors other than regular maintenance for a full calendar year. This will enable one to learn what grows in the community by studying both your own yard and your neighbors' properties. In particular, it is vital to understand where the summer sun infiltrates through the trees. At the same time, go for a walk in the surrounding woodlands to see what native plants are growing there. Don't dig them up, but make notes on what they are and when they bloom. Native plants, when acquired from a nursery, can be a great asset to your cottage garden, since they already grow in the area.

Finally, one should get down on their knees and sniff the ground at their cottage. Remember that the lovely smell of leaf loam from the decay of tree leaves means the soil is probably acidic. One can purchase a soil test kit to determine if this is true but should take a look around to see if acid-loving plants like rhododendron or mountain laurel have been planted nearby. If the soil is acidic, one will need to either identify specific plants that flourish in this environment or add material to the soil to change its consistency.

Finally, if one feels the urge to get their fingers dirty in the soil during their first year, pursue container gardening. Pot up some annuals and try them in various spots in the garden. If they are not tolerant of the shade, they can be easily moved to a new spot.

After that first year of watching, one can begin to make informed decisions about adding or subtracting plants. The first stop will be the foundational bushes and shrubs located next to the house and beneath the trees. Native mountain rhododendron is a favorite and are used extensively at Eagles Mere, Mount Gretna and many other Pennsylvania cottage communities. The plant is evergreen, hardy and blooms later than many modern hybrids. This is particularly important since the blooming season should ideally coincide with both one's residence and the summer program season. The native mountain rhododendrons are different from the recent hybrids sold today. The modern examples—and I can speak from personal experience—rarely have the stamina to handle the tough growing conditions and, often, lack of maintenance at summer cottages.

There are nurseries that exclusively sell the native plants, and I encourage gardeners to buy from those firms. Digging plants in the wild is not only bad for the plants and the environment, but in many areas, it is also illegal. Wild plants can also bring diseases and insects into a garden that will later have to be dealt with, so the better bet is to buy from an established grower.

Another kin plant to the rhododendron is the mountain laurel. The state flower of Pennsylvania, the mountain laurel is more delicate than its wild rhododendron cousin. As a result, it can be easily broken by people walking into it and thus needs to be in a more protected location. Its color is striking and can be found in a wide range of shades. They often bloom right after the rhododendrons and provide a nice continuum of color in the early part of the cottage season.

For the communities located near the shore, the rugosa rose is an ideal choice. A native of China, it has the ability to live close to salt water with seeming immunity to the salt air and occasional super storm. The rugosa is fast growing, and the thorny branches attract birds while dissuading marauding cats. The seeds, known as rose hips, can be made into jelly. The bushes are resistant to many of the mold, rust and blackspot strains that are common to hybrid roses, particularly along the hot and humid seashore. Finally, the rugosa is summer blooming, has a lovely fragrance and is the textbook definition for a seaside rose in appearance.

Another favorite for mountain or costal cottages is the butterfly bush. This plant grows robustly under all conditions and blooms consistently from spring to frost. Named because of the butterflies it attracts, the bush is a favorite among children of all ages. Butterfly bush blooms (say that three times quickly) can be cut for indoor use, although some people do not like their strong fragrance. The older varieties are usually deep purple in color and are today described in garden books as being muddy purple. For the experimenter, there are sturdy modern hybrids that can be found in a wide range of colors. It is important to always trim a butterfly bush back hard in spring in order to promote new flowers and growth. Without a trim, the bush will not produce as many blooms. Butterfly bushes reseed readily, so be aware that a single plant may grow into a clump within a short span of time.

For a non-blooming plant, one of the best traditional choices is the holly. They love acidic soils and are slow growing. The latter is noteworthy whenever you see a holly of great size, since it is a particularly ancient specimen. They are evergreen, so the branches can be cut for holiday decorating. In order to obtain berries, one needs to purchase both a male and female plant. Hollies are not the most child- or pet-friendly of plants, but they are beloved by birds.

My preference is to find a grower who stocks native hollies rather than the modern hybrids. The natives tend to grow larger and faster than the hybrids and are more historically accurate for cottage landscapes. Conversely, they tend to not be as thick in foliage. Finding native hollies is challenging, as they are not often sold by commercial greenhouses. A favorite greenhouse of mine in southern New Jersey keeps them in stock but hides them behind the greenhouse, as they are not as popular as the modern hybrids.

Perennial flowering plant choices are more limited than bushes and depend greatly on the amount of available shade. Lenten lilies and Solomon's seal are two ideal choices. The Lenten lilies bloom early in the spring (hence the name) and can continue well into the summer. They are evergreen, although late in the season, they will drop their leaves. Solomon's seal has a tremendous arching, blooming stalk that works well around a cottage. Plant both in groups of three and wait for them to spread out to create a thick groundcover.

For partially sunny gardens, day lilies and phlox are ideal choices. There are both native and hybrid species of both, and they will grow under the most adverse conditions if treated even moderately well. My preference among the two is the orange tawny day lily, also called the ditch lily in the South. It is easy to grow and can be planted either around trees or in stand-alone clumps. There are many modern hybrids of this plant, although the older varieties tend to be more aggressive in spreading. Phlox is the summer flower of choice in the Mid-Atlantic and can be planted around cottages for added color. The older varieties of phlox bloom in purple/pink and white. Like roses, phlox can develop mold during the height of August steaminess, so it's better to plant them in a location where there is ample air circulation.

Periwinkle is a lovely and carefree groundcover, and it can be fun for children to pick the blooms as miniature bouquets in the spring. English ivy is on my "DO NOT PLANT" list, as it is attractive to pests, and its tendrils can quickly destroy the exterior of a cottage. I have also seen pachysandra used with some cottages, but I find it about as exciting as shoe polish (no offense to shoe polish). Ferns can be lovely but seem to need the exact right conditions, which often means they have a high transplant failure rate. Remember, as with all native plants, don't dig up ferns from nature; buy them from a garden center.

Container gardening and statuary has become a way of dressing up cottage gardens, particularly in the summer. These gardens have the benefit of being portable, so changing their look is easy. It is important to carefully check the soil before replanting the subsequent year, as squirrels seem to love to hide acorns in vacant pots. For garden ornaments, the preferred choices are wind chimes, Mexican Talavera pottery planters and sundials. Birdbaths should be soft (worn concrete is ideal) and covered in moss. Bird feeders or houses should be natural and made of wood or gourds.

One plant that is a must-have for all summer cottages is the Boston fern. Having studied dozens of photographs from the 1900 to 1910 period, I have found that nearly every American home—summer or year-round—incorporated Boston ferns into their interior and exterior décor. They were immensely popular both for their ease of care and their use in flower arrangements. For summer cottages, they are particularly useful, as they can survive long periods without water. When selecting a Boston fern for the table or as a hanging pot, buy the largest plant you can. Small and skimpy plants rarely grow fast or large enough to make them worthwhile.

The front porch for modern cottage lovers remains the center of life for a household, just as it did one hundred years ago. Front porches, of course, should be populated with wicker furniture, repurposed bridge floor lamps and a large table. The latter was critical for playing games or reading the paper. And always resting on that table is a pitcher or mason jar that is filled with gladiolas. In Mount Gretna, the preferred source for such flowers is the elderly Mennonite lady and her family who set up in the parking lot adjacent to the camp meeting on Saturdays. She and her family have been there for decades, and they do a bumper business selling to the locals. So, why use gladiolas? Because they were once a sign of luxury. Each gladiola stalk grows from a single corm or bulb. Raising them requires considerable effort, since the grower has only one chance for a successful bloom and the flower stalk can easily be affected by wind or rain.

Lighting on a porch is a more recent phenomenon, since most cottage communities were exclusively used during the summer season, when daylight was at its longest. Overhead lighting is really a bit out of keeping with tradition, with most people preferring repurposed boudoir lamps or standing bridge lights. Chinese paper or cloth lanterns with bulbs in them are classically popular, although, today, one sees more LED Christmas lights on cottages.

Modernity has added many new features to cottage interiors. Bathrooms and laundry rooms are the most common of modern adaptions in cottages. Because of the plumbing constraints, both are usually positioned in some proximity to the kitchen to minimize running pipes and stacks. The best cottages have been able to hide these spaces in such a way that the overall floorplan of the house is kept as open as possible.

Shag carpeting became the cottage flooring choice beginning in the 1960s. Today, the aesthetic has changed, and people have flipped back to finished wood floors dotted with area rugs. The ideal choices are southwestern weavings, such as Navajo or Chimayo rugs. These are part of the Arts and Crafts aesthetic and can easily be rolled and stored with mothballs for the winter. There are many sources for these rugs, both new and used.

Cottage walls were constructed using either vertical bead board paneling or painted plaster, depending on the location of the cottage. Varnished knotty pine paneling is again a 1960s–80s feature that is probably not the greatest of choices aesthetically.

Some larger cottages had fireplaces or small camp stoves, especially those found in the North. Today, one can have such a stove fitted into a house easily. However, the caveat is always to let a professional install stoves or fireplaces, lest the cottage and then the entire community burn to the ground on a cold night. That said, there is something special about smelling wood burning in a fireplace on a fall day.

Cottage bedrooms have always been a challenge. Originally, they were only for sleeping and thus had sufficient room for just a small bed, washstand and, perhaps, a dresser. Today, we find such spaces claustrophobic, and as a result, many cottage owners knock out the thin partitions between small bedrooms to create fewer but larger rooms. Kitchens are often of the ship's galley variety with narrow spaces and apartment-scale appliances. As a result, some cottage owners have, with varying degrees of success, attempted to enlarge their cottages to accommodate modern spaces. When done thoughtfully and with sensitivity to the original structure, this can be very successful. Examples include building side or back additions for modern bathrooms and a kitchen. An interesting option, seen in a few of the more densely constructed cottage communities, has been to purchase the house next door and connect the two. If done well and zoning permits it, this can be very successful in gaining extra space. A less successful path is to close in the front porch to create the incongruous Florida room that usually becomes the catch-all for everything from holiday decorations to boxes of bleach.

The recent shift to use cottages year-round has also created challenges for owners who wish to winterize their properties. When cottages were used only in the summer, a custodian for the community association would come in the fall to turn off water service to cottages, thus preventing frozen pipes. That same custodian also would check on the houses during the winter for animal infestations or snow damage, and they would keep the surrounding pathways clear in case of fire. Today, with more year-round use of cottages, winter care falls more to the individual property owner. Cottage owners who want to live in their cottages in the winter need to develop a plan to prevent sewer or water pipes from freezing. I recall a contractor friend telling me that I just needed to feed heat tape down the toilet stack to prevent freezing. The idea seemed bizarre, and I ignored the advice, suffering through three frozen and burst sewer stacks before realizing that his approach had been right.

Electrical service is one of those items that does need to be checked and upgraded when you purchase a cottage. While knob and tube wiring is not the instantaneous fire danger that modern electricians have led us to believe, it should be replaced and upgraded. The risk with most cottages and electric service beyond trees falling on wires outside has been wayward squirrels eating wiring inside the house. Gaining access to attics, they can wreak havoc on walls, wires and Christmas decorations.

Finally, there is the question of whether large air conditioning units are appropriate for cottage living. Historically speaking, families went away to their cottages to escape the heat of the city. They relied on sleeping porches, which were usually second-floor screened porches where the family slept outdoors in hot weather. While this is romantic to consider, there must have been many steamy August nights when no one slept well. Today, air conditioning can solve these problems. While some would say window units are unsightly and noisy, they are a bit more honest to my eye, and they can be removed more readily than large outdoor units, thus providing a better look for the cottage. Similarly, there is a debate about how cottages should be heated in the winter. Wood stoves are charming but risky because of the density of surrounding residences. Electric baseboards are the most passive in terms of impact, but they can be costly. Oil or propane tanks seem to be popular for many houses today, with some families doing a lot to camouflage these from view while others plunk them down pretty much anywhere.

Furnishing the modern cottage is very much an open field of consideration. Shabby chic or cottagecore are, of course, the favored styles. By definition, these informal styles use older furnishings to create a soft and lived-in look. Cottages were originally furnished using older items from their owners' attics, so the look has always been there. Today, however, fewer people have their grandmother's attic to raid for furnishings, so families pivot to haunting antique malls and flea markets. The important part about shabby chic is that the items need to make sense and work as part of the décor. A bit of wit and humor is, in fact, a key element. Thus, an ancient taxidermy deer head decorated with a clown nose, Santa hat and Christmas lights paints the perfect whimsical touch.

Cottages are small informal dwellings, so large case pieces of furniture rarely fit inside. Big sideboards or giant club sofas are definitely bad choices. Wicker, preferably vintage, is perfect for the outside porch and can be used inside. In tribute to real or mythical elderly relatives, there has to be at least one rocking chair on the porch.

Inside, occasional tables and lamps with heavy shades and a discrete bar cabinet are all good choices. For those who wish to go hardcore, one can acquire taxidermy, framed leave collages and seashells to create a natural feel for the interior. Brass or iron beds work well, as do recycled and refinished bedroom suites. The furniture of the Great Depression (1930s) is a particularly good choice, as it is available, inexpensive and historically fits into the cottage look. As a rule, furnishings should mix and complement but definitely not match. Curtains in the windows should be both consistent with the period of the cottages and provide privacy.

Fires, floods and wind damage are parts of life everywhere, but they can be particularly destructive for cottage communities. Nearly every camp meeting and Chautauqua has a story of some natural disaster that destroyed part of the community. One of the most challenged has been Island Grove Camp Meeting in Mexico, Pennsylvania, as it has suffered from both fires and floods. Rebuilt and still functioning, it is a tribute to the tenacity of its residents.

Fire was the most feared of natural disasters in cottage communities. Mount Lebanon, Mount Gretna Campmeeting and Chester Heights all had serious fires that destroyed parts of their communities. One fire in Mount Gretna resulted in the loss of eleven cottages, and the area in which they stood remains vacant as painful testimony to destructive power of fire. The shifting demographic to year-round residency has both helped and hindered fire prevention. The positive is that most of the communities have people living there year-round, thus fires can be detected. The negative is that many of these cottage communities are located in townships where building codes and enforcement have been lacking. As a result, repairs have been made by amateurs rather than licensed professional contractors.

Despite all of this talk about disasters, hopefully you are now thinking about becoming part of a cottage community. If so, my first advice is to take the time to identify a community that shares your values and views. Second, do your homework about how and when cottages are put on the market. The cottage real estate market has changed dramatically because of the stay-at-home-work movement following the COVID-19 pandemic. Ironically, what attracted the original builders—unique buildings, great cultural life and minimal upkeep—is just as appealing to many people today. The difference is that most are now considering cottages for year-round living. It is important to remember though that visiting a spot is a lot different than living there. Cottage living is not for everyone. Perhaps the biggest issue with modern cottage living is that residents better know and love their neighbors, since they are only about three feet away. They will hear and know of every fight, disagreement and make-up in your house. Further, because cottage communities are frequent destinations for tourists and day-trippers, one has to accept a certain degree of public scrutiny for your decorating choices. I recall falling asleep on the porch of my cottage at Mount Gretna and being awakened by two people chastising us for not having an American flag flying from the house. Front porch living is a two-way mirror.

11

THE FUTURE OF COTTAGES

O ver the last few decades, I have visited dozens of cottage communities in the Mid-Atlantic. Despite having been founded within twenty years of each other, they are remarkably disparate. Eagles Mere, Chautauqua, Lily Dale, Ocean Grove and South Seaville remain remarkably true to their original missions. They have evolved in their operations, but their core beliefs remain remarkably true. Families still pass their cottages on to the next generation, although there are also a remarkably high number of new residents who buy into the community. Real estate values have remained stable and have actually grown because of the paucity of cottages that appear on the market.

At the opposite extreme is a community like Marantha Camp Meeting in Montgomery County, Pennsylvania, whose cottages were bulldozed in 1988. The news coverage of the destruction of this once-vibrant camp meeting noted that the program had shut down some years before. "It's a blighted area with a lot of dilapidated homes" said Commissioner Paul B. Bartle in an October 2, 2021 article by staff writers for the *Allentown Morning Call*. Today, little remains of what was once a large camp meeting consisting of a tabernacle, 120 cottages, a hotel and a gymnasium. In Ephrata, Pennsylvania, the aforementioned Camp Silver Belle failed several decades after its founder died. The costs of maintaining the old Victorian hotel coupled with a declining interest in spiritualism led to the spiritualist camp's demise. Ironically, the hotel lingered long after the camp closed, begging for a buyer, but when none could be found, it was razed.

In between these extremes are the cottage communities that have struggled to adapt to the changing modern world. Mount Lebanon, Malaga and Brandywine Station all continue to offer summer camp meeting programs in the traditions of their respective pasts. An aging and waning attendance has resulted in struggles to identify relevant programs that would attract new participants. As families age and children move on, many cottages go wanting for care.

A fourth group are the communities that have held on to aspects of their former identify but have moved in a more secular direction. Mount Gretna Chautauqua and Mount Gretna Campmeeting have found a new and popular appeal for their programs through organizations like Gretna Theater. While keeping their roots, they have found modern relevancy and are thus growing.

Finally, there are the communities like Pitman and Chester Heights, which have changed their missions dramatically. Pitman is now a purely year-round residential community with no ties to any church or camp meeting tradition. Chester Heights, at the time of this writing, totters on the edge of survival. There have been dramatic efforts to convert the community into a church retreat center, although outside economic conditions cast that future in doubt.

Looking at the range of different cottage communities, one can truly generalize and call them a modern anachronism. They are like the Roman god Janus, who was depicted on ancient coins as having two faces. One is looking forward to the future while the other is looking back to the past. The cottage communities are very much tied to a past in which summers were about going away to refresh the body and pursue spiritual or intellectual enlightenment or learning. Governance of the community was vested in civic leaders who thoughtfully managed the community's assets and ensured it provided both the physical and moral/intellectual growth for its members. As the communities have aged, however, the world around them has also changed. They were all born in the era of the wooden water pump, the horse-drawn carriage and light from a gas fixture or kerosene lamp. They now exist in a modern world that is both consistently changing and making demands on communities. New building codes, charging stations for electric cars and the need for internet service must be constantly addressed. To fail to do so is to risk the loss of the next generation of the community.

As a result, the governance of the communities has also had to evolve. There is no single universal playbook for the associations to follow in making decisions. Nowhere is this more evident than in the issue of land use and ownership. The cottage associations, particularly the camp meetings, were established on a model whereby the community (through the formal association) holds all the real estate in trust. This included all the land in common areas, such as parks and the surrounding grazing and recreational property. And most importantly, the property beneath all the cottages. Revenue to support the association comes not only from admissions to the various programs but also from ground leases to the residents and vendors. Unfortunately, this becomes a finite pot of money, especially if there is little interest or motivation to raise the rent.

In many respects, present-day cottage communities will have to learn to function like a modern homeowners' association. Tradition, however, remains the governing principal for many, so a great many still follow governance strictures dating to the 1890s. As an example, a modern member of a homeowners' association who fails to make repairs or keep up their property can face any number of penalties, including civil litigation. Old cottage communities lack this ability to enforce their rules, so their solution has been and continues to be peer shaming. This is effective so long as the strength of the community members exists to put pressure on recalcitrant members to make repairs and regulate and ensure the safety and happiness of everyone.

The key to this peer pressure strategy rested in the ability of the governing association to determine exactly who could purchase a property. This system was, and is, an effective way to regulate the residents and build that peer network to ensure the vitality of the community. To an outsider, such a process seems rather "big brother"–like, but in fact, it is now ensuring communities remain strong. The process has several components. First among the camp meetings is a profession of faith that includes membership in the church and sometimes in the camp meeting itself. This is followed by agreeing to the rules of the community, usually by a legal or sometimes informal document. Rarely—although not unheard of—a vote is required for admission. Once approved, one can either purchase a lot and house or lease the ground and construct a house.

The terms of ground leases are generally long and the rents low, which are positives. However, the leases also mean that getting bank financing is extremely challenging. Therefore, renters better have cash in hand and be ready to settle. Disposing of a cottage is equally complex, since the steps need to be worked sequentially in reverse. All of this means lengthy coordination with various parties, which does not always fit well in our modern era of instant gratification.

Another interesting wrinkle is what do you do if you have a cottage but don't like the real estate. Well, you can move it. There are numerous cases in which families have moved their cottages to different lots in the community. Sometimes, this is done to move to a spot that is higher and drier than others because of summer rain flooding. In other cases, people want to be closer to the tabernacle. In any case, a local builder can be hired to jack up the house and skid the building to its new location. Metaphorically, one is picking up their tent (or, in this case, cottage) and pitching camp in a better spot.

A great deal of authority for the success of the community rests on the local association's board. In the past, these have been made up of leading local figures who were well known and had a common vision for the community. What they lacked in practical understanding about money or land use, they more than made up for in passion and commitment. By the 1950s, however, these well-intentioned boards came up against the complexities of zoning, public utility infrastructure and building codes. An example during the 1970s was when Mount Lebanon Camp Meeting ran into issues with the state about its land use. After much review, restrictions were imposed on how many year-round residents were allowed in the community.

Because of the incredible density of houses (often only three feet apart), there is also a substantial risk that a fire or building collapse at one property can spill over into neighboring houses. Recently, I saw a cottage that had multiple trees growing on top of its roof. The combined weight of the plants, dirt and moisture had buckled the porch, and the house was in danger of collapse. A good windstorm was all it would take to end the story of that house—plus that of the neighboring house that would be hit by the debris. Sadly, the association board had nothing in its by-laws to demand the owner to make repairs, and the peer pressure factor was long gone.

One solution for associations has been to end leasing and sell the ground outright to owners with deed restrictions. This approach has the advantage of ensuring cottage owners have a stake in maintaining their property. Thus, everyone has skin in the proverbial game of preserving the community. While this sounds very effective and business-like, this model does have its challenges. These communities exist because of their historic commitments to religion, education and belief. That history is difficult to quantify in modern legal documents, and this gives rise to misunderstandings. An example of this is a camp meeting that allowed the open purchase of cottages without any interview of the buyers. The result was a lawsuit filed within a year by a couple who did not like the noise of the evangelical Sunday services. Their claim was based on their deed that had a covenant allowing for quiet enjoyment of their property. The suit was filed insofar as the couple felt that the Sunday morning and evening services violated that part of their agreement. For the rest of the community, this was an outrage, since the camp meeting's sole purpose was for religious education and services. It was an ugly and unfortunate episode that highlighted the potential risk of losing the core identity of a cottage community.

For those cottage communities that do remain true to their core of learning and belief, they have nearly unlimited opportunities to grow. A *Washington Post* article from July 2023 on the mother Chautauqua in New York provides a useful modern listing of political figures who have visited in the last decades. The list begins with President Bill Clinton, who arguably channeled the political savvy of Roosevelt. He came to Chautauqua to prepare for his political debate with challenger Bob Dole in the 1996 campaign. Supreme Court justices Ruth Bader Ginsburg and Robert H. Jackson have also been frequent speakers. The article then addressed the most notorious of incidents to have struck any cottage community program: the stabbing of author Salman Rushdie at Chautauqua in 2022. While the court case for the accused in this incident has yet to start, it is clear that the attack shook the community to its core. There is a love of learning but at what physical price to the lecturer and the attendees?

Over the last two decades, the internet has become the place where you can go to watch 24/7 lecture-based programming on a host of topics ranging across the political and religious spectrum. The popularity of these programs is immense, and I recall binge watching a number myself while stuck inside during the 2020 COVID closures. So, if these were so popular, why would anyone want to attend a program with Justice Ginsburg or Salman Rushdie? Because they are following that innate human desire to share such experiences with others. Saying that, however, does not answer the other fundamental question about why people would go to hear a politician, writer or philosopher rather than an actor, comic or musician. At its heart, all the cottage communities were about learning. It was the pleasure derived from growing spiritually and mentally that drove people to the program. As one summer resident in Chautauqua New York described, the program was "National Public Radio camp for grown-ups."

Whatever the motivation, the summer cottage communities have and will arguably continue to play an important role in the intellectual life of our nation. They will serve as places where attendees can gather, perhaps originally as strangers and then later as friends, to engage in that core desire to enjoy summer vacations while growing both intellectually and spiritually.

NOTES

1. Rivinus and Biddle, *Lights along the Delaware*, 84.
2. Ibid., 14.
3. Henry David Thoreau, *Walden* (Reprint, London: Macmillan Collector's Library, 2016), uncited pages from online extract.
4. See National Spiritualist Association of Churches, "Directory of Churches and Camps," https://nsac.org/directory/churches.
5. James and James, *Mere Reflections*, 19.
6. McFarland, *Eagles Mere and the Sullivan Highlands*, 27.
7. Meck, *First City Zouaves and City Grays*.
8. See Wilson, "From the Fountain."
9. Senate On-line Directory.
10. *The Story of the Jubilee Singers with Their Songs African American Singers of Fisk University* (London: Hodder and Stoughton, 1875), 1–35.
11. Harrison, *Culture Under Canvas*, 251.
12. Eastlack, *Gloucester County in the Eighteen-Fifties*, 77.
13. Huttar and Huttar, *Island Grove Camp Meeting*, 54.
14. Moore, *Ida Norton*, 22–23.
15. Wilson, *Annual Report*, 101.
16. Tarbell, *All in the Day's Work*, 68.
17. Downing, *Architecture of Country Houses*, 10.
18. Ibid., 11.
19. Ibid., 105.
20. Reed, *Cottage Houses*, 130.

SELECTED BIBLIOGRAPHY

Aron, Cindy. *Working at Play: A History of Vacations in the United States*. New York: Oxford University Press, 1999.

Bachelder, John B. *Popular Resorts, and How to Reach Them*. Boston, MA: John B. Bachelder Publishing, 1874.

Bitner, Jack. *Mount Gretna: A Coleman Legacy*. Lebanon, PA: Blylet Offset, 1990.

Brown, Kenneth O. *Holy Ground, Too: The Camp Meeting Family Tree*. Hazelton, PA: Holiness Archives, 1997.

Case, Victoria, and Robert Case. *We Called It Culture: The Story of Chautauqua*. New York: Doubleday and Company, 1948.

Chaee, Rebecca. *Chautauqua Summer*. New York: Harcourt Brace, 1993.

Colt, George Howe. *The Big House: A Century in the Life of an American Summer Home*. New York: Scribner, 2003.

Conkling, Edgar. *Frederick Law Olmsted's Point Chautauqua*. Buffalo, NY: Canisius Press, 2001.

Crocker, Kathleen. *Chautauqua Institution*. Charleston, SC: Arcadia Publishing, 2001.

Curtin, Merle. *The Growth of American Thought*. 3rd ed. New York: Harper and Row, 1964.

Dagnall, Sarah. *Martha's Vineyard Camp Meeting Association*. Martha's Vineyard, MA: Martha's Vineyard Camp Meeting Association, 1985.

Danielson, Robert A. *Tenting by the Cross: The History and Development of the Methodist and Holiness Camp Meeting*. Wilmore, KY: First Fruits/Asbury Theological Seminary, 2019.

DeBoll, Irene Briggs. *Recollections of the Lyceum and Chautauqua Circuits.* Freeport, ME: Bond Wainwright Company, 1969.

Dolan, Michael. *The American Porch: An Informal History of an Informal Place.* Guilford, CT: Lyons Press, 2002.

Downing, A.J. *The Architecture of County Houses: Designs for Cottages, Farm Houses and Villas.* New York: Appleton and Company, 1853.

Eastlack, John Cawman. *Gloucester County in the Eighteen-Fifties: Being the Diary of John Cawman Eastlack.* Gloucester, NJ: Gloucester County Historical Society Publications, 1952.

Edwards, J.T. *The Silva of Chautauqua Lake, N.Y.* Meadville, PA: Flood and Vincent, 1892.

Fischer, David Hackett. *Albion's Seed: Four British Folkways in America.* New York: Oxford University Press, 1989.

Gorman, B.W. *Camp Meeting Manual.* Boston, MA: Edward B. Degen, 1854.

Gould, Joseph E. *The Chautauqua Movement.* Albany, NY: SUNY Press, 1972.

Grimes, John Franklin. *The Romance of the American Camp Meeting.* Cincinnati, OH: Caxton Press, 1922.

Harrison, Harry P. *Culture Under Canvas: The Story of Tent Chautauqua.* New York: Hastings House, 1958.

Hines, Sarah H. *Cottage Communities: The American Camp Meeting Movement.* Ashland, MA: Hines Art Press, 2015.

Holdcraft, Paul E. *History of the Pennsylvania Conference of the Church of the United Brethren in Christ.* Fayetteville, PA: Craft Press Inc., 1938.

Hoover, Stephanie. *Philadelphia Spiritualists: The Curious Case of Katie King.* Charleston, SC: The History Press, 2013.

Huttar, Charles A., and Joy C. Huttar. *Island Grove Camp Meeting.* Mifflintown, PA: Juniata County Historical Society, 1999.

James, Barbara, and Bush James. *Mere Reflections: A Unique Journey through Historic Eagles Mere.* Mountoursville, PA: Paulhamus, 1988.

Kuhlig, Verna Kathryn. *Spiritualist Lyceum Manual.* New York: National Spiritualist Association, 1993.

Maclean, A. *Penuel, Or Face to Face with God.* New York: W.C. Palmer, 1869.

Mason, Bernard S. *Cabins, Cottages and Summer Houses.* New York: S.A. Barnes and Company, 1947.

McFarland, J. Horace. *Eagles Mere and Sullivan Highlands.* Harrisburg, PA: Telegraph Press, 1944.

Meck, Charles P. *First City Zouaves and City Grays: History of Harrisburg's Leading Military Organization, 1861–1913.* Harrisburg PA: Telegraph Press, 1917.

Meredith, Thomas R. *The Mount Gretna Campmeeting Association.* Mount Gretna, PA: Mount Gretna Campmeeting Association, 1992.

Moore, H.H. *Ida Norton or Life at Chautauqua.* Jamestown, NY: M. Bailey, 1878.

Morrison, Theodore. *Chautauqua: A Center for Education, Religion and the Arts in America.* Chicago, IL: University of Chicago Press, 1974.

Nagy, Ron. *The Spirts of Lily Dale.* Lakeville, NC: Galde Press, 2013.

O'Hara, Gerald. *Ethel Post Parrish: Mediumship in America.* New York: KDP/Amazon, 2020.

Osborn, Lucy B. *In the Beginning God: Pioneer Days of Ocean Grove.* New York: Methodist Book Council, 1917.

Ptacin, Mira. *The In-Betweens: The Spiritualists, Mediums and Legends of Camp Etna.* New York: Norton, 2019.

Reed, S.B. *Cottage Houses for Village and Country Homes.* New York: Orange Judd Company, 1895.

Reieser, Andrew. *The Chautauqua Movement: Protestants, Progressives and the Culture of Modern Liberalism.* New York: Columbia, 2003.

Rivinus, Marion Willis, and Katherine Biddle. *Lights along the Delaware.* Philadelphia, PA: Dorrance and Company, 1965.

Scharff, Robert. *Complete Summer Home Handbook.* New York: Prentice Hall, 1952.

Schropp, Michael. *Mount Gretna…A Postcard History.* Lebanon, PA: Lebanon News, 1977.

Schultz, James R. *The Romance of Small-Town Chautauquas.* Columbia: University of Missouri Press, 2002.

Seybert, Henry. *Preliminary Report of the Commission Appointed by the Univ. of Pennsylvania to Investigate Modern Spiritualism.* Philadelphia, PA: Lippincott Company, 1887.

Shellenberger, Melanie. *High Country Summers: The Early Second Homes of Colorado.* Tucson: University of Arizona Press, 2012.

Smith, Jean Jacoby. *An Altar in the Forest: A History of Mount Lebanon Camp Meeting.* Lebanon, PA: Blyler's Offset Press, 1990.

Sullivan, A. *A Time to Remember: A History of New Jersey Methodist's First Camp Meeting South Seaville, New Jersey.* Chelsea, MI: Book Crafters, 1988.

Tapia, John. *Circuit Chautauqua.* Harrisburg, PA: McFarland and Company, 1997.

Tarbell, Ida M. *All in the Day's Work.* New York: Macmillan Company, 1939.

United States Senate On-line Directory of Members of the Senate. https://www.senate.gov/senators.

Van Slyck, Abigail. *A Manufactured Wilderness; Summer Camps and the Shaping of American Youth*. Minneapolis: University of Minnesota Press, 2006.

Vincent, John M. *The Chautauqua Movement*. Boston, MA: Chautauqua Press, 1886.

Weiss, Ellen. *City in the Woods*. Boston, MA: Northeastern University Press, 1987.

Wilson, Harold F. *Annual Report: Ocean Grove Camp Meeting*. Ocean Grove, NJ: Published by Order of the Ocean Grove Camp Meeting, various years.

———. "From the Fountain." Jigger Shop. https://jiggershop.com/sundaes.

———. *A History of Pitman, New Jersey*. York, PA: Maple Press, 1976.

INDEX

Pennsylvania National Guard 46,
  93, 124
Pennsylvania Railroad 26, 93, 100
Pentecostal Marantha Camp
  Meeting 77
periwinkle 150
Philadelphia 15, 16, 30, 46, 52, 74,
  80, 91, 100, 102
phlox 150
Pickett, LaSalle "Sally" 61
picnic housekeeping 132
Pitman Camp Meeting 87
Pittsburgh, Titusville and Buffalo
  Railroad 43
Post, Ethel 114
Princess Silver Belle 116
Putnam Cottage 24

Q

Quakers 16, 108
Queen Victoria 105

R

Redpath 58, 62
Redpath-Vawter 57
Reed, S.B. 138
rhododendron 148, 149
Roddenberry, Gene 120
Roosevelt, Franklin Delano 38

S

Scott, A.E. 50
Sears and Roebuck Company 121

Second Great Awakening 21, 68,
  69, 105, 107, 108
shabby chic 132, 153
Shingle Style 139
Sinclair, Upton 121
Skeyhill, Tom 61
Smith, Joseph 107
Solomon's seal 150
South Seaville Camp Meeting 84
spiritualism 23, 104, 107, 108, 109,
  110, 112, 115, 116, 119, 156
Spiritualist Camp at Freeville, New
  York 118
Spiritualists' National Union 109
Stephan, John and Mary 114
Stoverdale Camp Meeting 47
Sullivan Highlands 31, 34
Sunday, Billy 72
Swarthmore 58
Swatara Creek 93

T

Taft, William Howard 18
Tarbell, Ida 121, 132
Thoreau, Henry David 19
Truth, Sojourner 108, 115
Twain, Mark 120

V

Vincent, John Heyl 40, 41, 129

W

Washington Post 160

ABOUT THE AUTHOR

Peter Swift Seibert has lived and worked in some of the coolest places in the United States. Born in Harrisburg, Pennsylvania, he began his career in museums as the executive director for the Historical Society of Dauphin County at the ripe old age of twenty-one. Four years later, he moved to Lancaster as the CEO of the Heritage Center of Lancaster County. Over the next fifteen years, he was also an adjunct faculty member at Penn State University and the Pennsylvania College of Art and Design, and he wrote two books. His career then pivoted south to College Park, Maryland, where he was CEO of the National Council for History Education. Being inspired by Horace Greeley, he looked west and became the CEO of the Millicent Rogers Museum in Taos, New Mexico. Missing the land of humidity and hurricanes, he moved back east to Colonial Williamsburg for several years. Then recruited back west, he and his family headed to Cody, Wyoming, where he served a stint as the president of the Buffalo Bill Center of the West. Today, he is the CEO and president of the Independence Seaport Museum in Philadelphia. He is a thirty-plus-year columnist for *Antiques and Auction News* and serves on numerous museum and patriotic society boards. He is currently the board president of PA Museums, the professional organization of museums in Pennsylvania. When he isn't busy haunting antique shops and visiting Chautauquas, he tends his garden.